An Examined Faith

An Examined Faith

The Grace of Self-Doubt

James M. Gustafson

Fortress Press
Minneapolis

For

Richard R. Niebuhr
Gordon D. Kaufman
Van A. Harvey

AN EXAMINED FAITH
The Grace of Self-Doubt

Scripture quotations from the New Revised Standard Version of the Bible are copyright © 1989 by the Division of Christian Education of the National Council of the Churches of Christ in the United States of America and are used by permission.

Cover image: © Mick Tarel/Photodisc. Used by permission.
Cover design: Kevin van der Leek Design, Inc.
Book design: Ann Delgehausen

ISBN: 0-8006-3628-7

The paper used in this publication meets the minimum requirements of American National Standard for Information Sciences—Permanence of Paper for Printed Library Materials, ANSI Z329.48-1984.

Manufactured in the U.S.A.
08   07   06   05   04   2   3   4   5   6   7   8   9   10

Contents

From the cowardice that dares not face new truth
From the laziness that is contented with half truth
From the arrogance that thinks it knows all truth,
Good Lord, deliver [us].

This prayer from Kenya, which is quoted twice more, points to the principal theological and ethical issue of this book, and expresses the passion which moved me to write it. No Christian in parts of the earth that are saturated with scientific and other secular knowledge can avoid the impact of alternative ways to describe, explain, value, and give meaning to natural and historical events and human actions. Biblical or theological language is seldom the first that theologians, pastors, and church members use to understand issues of health and disease, politics and international affairs, personal anguish and fear, violence in marriages and between nations, poverty and interracial tensions, etc. We use vocabulary, concepts, and arguments currently available from our culture. The scientific and other secular information, concepts, and modes of argument available to us are diverse; a behaviorist explanation of human activity differs from a Freudian, an economist's explanation of human activity is based on very different premises from a Kantian moral philosopher's, the violence in "the Holy Land" is explained and justified differently by Palestinians and Israelis. And certainly religious voices are not harmonized: some reject secular accounts if they threaten Christian beliefs that are held dogmatically; some seek to revise religious accounts in the light of scientific information and explanations; most find a way to accommodate, usually implicitly, their religious thought and life to biological, economic, psychological, political, philosophical, and literary interpretations that intersect religious ones.

Natural and historical events, human nature and activity, and even the Bible are places in which different disciplines intersect. Christian scholars continue to seek to smoothly direct traffic where historical and literary-critical disciplines meet their theological and religious interests in the Bible. Decades of articles and books about "the historical Jesus" are clearly only one case in point. So, also, are individual and social experiences: Is guilt caused, and therefore explained, by sin? Or by repressive parental nurturing of children, etc.?

This book does not focus primarily on epistemological issues between philosophers of theology and religion and philosophers of science. Abstract discussions can direct the intersecting traffic only in principle, and not in the thickets of particular public policy, or medical and other studies. This book does not offer another historical interpretation of the effects of the reviled Enlightenment on human cultures and activities. The distinction between revealed and natural theology is part of the problem, not part of the solution. Rather, in a way which could be refined and documented by empirical studies, it assumes that academic theologians, clergy, and laity *experience* in their day-to-day living, dissonant interpretations of their personal lives, their social relations, and political and social events. These people are also religious. If I were a young sociologist of religion, I would design a research project which would seek information about how religious professional and lay persons have dealt with, even if by denial, the effects on their traditional religious beliefs and practices from scientific and other secular disciplines. What intellectual problems *out there* are also personal issues *in us*. Resolutions of dissonance by theologians, ethicists, philosophers in learned papers and scholarly books do not settle conflicts in the minds of self-critical religious people.

Some, but not all, of the questions I raised in "Just what is 'postliberal' theology?" in the *Christian Century* in March 1999 are developed here. William Placher answered my question in a subsequent issue, and in an exchange that followed in April.

This book is the outcome of many years of varied academic and other experiences. From the beginning of my professional life I have been interested in the nontheological explanations of what theologians and ethicists also interpret. The question of my first book was, Can the continuity and unity of the Christian church be explained by sociological concepts? Much of it can. So how does a theological interpretation relate to that? Throughout my professional life I have been seriously engaged with persons from various disciplines and professions that intersect my ethical and theological concerns. In the summer of 1956, I was invited to do a policy study for Standard Oil Corporation, New Jersey. The principal issue was whether cost reduction could be achieved without unfairness to the workers: a conflict between utility and justice. To make my analysis relevant to the circumstance in which the issue arose I read the efficiency analyses of thirty-three oil barges and ten tugboats in the New York Harbor, spent several days on the barges and tugboats, and interviewed people from harbor personnel to middle managers, to board members of the international corporation and its subsidiary, Esso, which ran inland water transportation of

oil. Social ethics done only at abstract conceptual levels, or even through middle axioms, leaves a huge gap between theory, quantified information, and the
role obligations of persons. I have tried to understand events and issues from
the perspectives of other disciplines, and the many obligations of institutions
and their personnel. I have always reflected on implications of such experiences, and the disciplines involved, for my academic work and my life.

At the University of Chicago I taught with colleagues in several parts of the
university beyond my primary concentration in the Divinity School. Most of my
intellectual friendships were with secular colleagues. As Chair of the Midwest
Section of the American Academy of Arts and Sciences I was responsible for developing research and academic discourse on issues that are addressed by many
different scholars, for example, the business corporation in American society,
and, during the Cold War, "Is it immoral to *threaten* to use nuclear weapons?" At
the Hastings Center I was one of a group which, in the late sixties, developed
seminars and research on the legal, moral, and social implications of the rapid
developments in human genetics. I also served on the Advisory Committee to
the Director of the National Institutes of Health, and on the review committees
that examined proposals for research on human beings in the biological and the
social sciences. In these, and other engagements, I learned as much as possible,
and as was relevant, about the primary disciplines involved. In *Ethics from a
Theocentric Perspective*, two volumes, this cross-disciplinary work deeply affected my development of theology and ethics, as was quickly pointed out by
critics.

After thirty-three years, almost evenly divided between the faculties of Yale
and the University of Chicago, I was invited by a selection committee, and President James T. Laney, of Emory University, to conduct seminars for faculty
members from the professional schools and Arts and Sciences on topics related
to ethics. Optimally, each participant was relieved of teaching and administra-
tive obligations for a fourteen-week semester. The program was sponsored by
the Luce Endowment, but required even more resources from Emory. I selected
themes addressed by the many disciplines: human being/being human, nature,
responsibility (causal, etc.; not only moral), and the processes of describing, explaining, and valuing in various academic fields. During the eight years of the
program I read at least 350 books suggested by participants, and three times
each of the hundred, or so, that were used during the seminar sessions. About
ninety members of the Emory faculty participated, and others were involved
during an abbreviated program for two more years. All of the professional
schools were represented, and only chemistry and mathematics of the Arts and
Sciences were not. During these years my private agenda was the theme of this
book: How do I, as a theologian and ethicist, relate all of these ideas both to
Christian theology and ethics as disciplines, and to my own beliefs and living?
I read far, far more books outside of theology and ethics during those years
than materials that were my primary focus during previous decades. The most

central question of the seminars, though not always consciously addressed, was how do disciplines which intersect on a similar, if not the same, reality relate to each other? In this book I have focused that question on my principal areas of intellectual competence, theology and ethics, with one chapter of careful analysis of writings that have addressed my agenda. It is, however, only one example of scores of possible inquiries.

It is possible to acknowledge only those institutions and persons who have contributed to the development of this book, not all I recall from over four decades of academic life.

The president of Princeton Theological Seminary, Thomas W. Gillespie, and its faculty, honored me with an invitation to deliver the Benjamin Warfield Lectures on the Reformed Tradition in theology. I was given ample time to prepare for delivery, in March 2002, six lectures under the title "Theology and Ethics, and Other Disciplines." The invitation was a strong incentive to verbally express some of my thinking. The first three chapters have been only slightly revised from their lecture form; the fourth and fifth have been totally rewritten. Professor Daniel Migliore deserves special thanks for his interest, his encouragement to a heterodox Reformed theologian, and his gracious hospitality.

Uppsala University and Professor Carl-Reinhold Bråkenhielm invited me to return once more to Sweden to lecture during a conference on the topic "The Relevance of Theology," celebrating the centennial of Nathan Söderblom's appointment to the faculty, and his distinguished academic and ecclesial career. The lecture form of the final chapter is published in Carl-Reinhold Bråkenhielm and Gunhild Winqvist Hollman, eds., *The Relevance of Theology: Nathan Söderblom and the Development of an Academic Discipline* (Uppsala: Uppsala University, Uppsala Studies in Faiths and Ideologies 11, Acta Universitatis Upaliensis 2002), 101–11 (ISBN 91-554-5498-4). It is revised for use here by permission of the editors.

The materials in the second chapter have been used for several lectures and faculty seminars, depending on the focus of each invitation: as Phi Beta Kappa visiting scholar at nine colleges, as annual Phi Beta Kappa lecturer at Emory, Louisiana State universities, and other institutions; most recently at the University of Virginia at the invitation of my esteemed former student, James F. Childress, and at Baylor University, where I was pleased to deliver the first Daniel B. McGee Lecture, honoring the remarkably effective, multifaceted career of Professor McGee as teacher, author, churchman, faculty leader, and public citizen. The lectureship is endowed by Mr. Lyndon Olson and his wife; he is a businessman and former U.S. ambassador to Sweden whose life and work is deeply influenced by the person and teaching of Daniel McGee. That material and others similar to it were used through the years of my Emory senior honors seminar for undergraduates: a group annually selected from nominations by faculty from various departments. No doctoral seminar I ever conducted was livelier than it.

Special gratitude is due to four persons. The subtitle of the book comes, with generous permission, from Professor Margaret Farley of Yale. The phrase is from "Ethics, Ecclesiology and the Grace of Self-Doubt" in James J. Walter, Timothy O'Connell, and Thomas A. Shannon, eds., *A Call to Fidelity: On the Moral Theology of Charles E. Curran* (Washington, D.C.: Georgetown University Press, 2002), 55–75; see especially 66–70. An apt phrase is only one of Margaret Farley's contributions to my life and thought. She also read the first four Warfield Lectures, and guided some revisions.

Professor William Schwieker, of the University of Chicago also read the first four lectures, and his remarks made clear to me what I did *not* want to do; a decisive moment.

Professor Charles Swezey, of Union Theological Seminary, Richmond, has been a devoted friend and colleague for decades whose ability to empathize with my thinking has helped me to express it more clearly. During the preparation for the Warfield Lectures he critically analyzed all of them, and in intense exchanges aided my revision of the fifth and sixth. His intense work for many hours corrected awkward phrasings and many errors in this manuscript during what was to have been a week of holiday.

Finally, there is no way to enumerate the contributions of the participants in the Luce Faculty Seminars at Emory. I readily recall particular contributions of many of them without denigrating the collective impact of each seminar. Very few of those colleagues and friends will ever see this book, not to mention read it. For those intellectually exciting years on which I embarked at age sixty-three, special acknowledgment is due to James T. Laney, a former student, colleague, and friend, who as president invited me and sustained me, and to Provost Billy Frye, an atheistic biologist, who was a personal friend and institutional supporter, but more, an engaged intellectual interlocutor during hours of sipping margaritas and eating nachos in a local pub.

Introduction

The Issues and Their Importance

General Introduction and Agenda

On March 19, 1737, Jonathan Edwards wrote the following, in a letter to Scotland. Edwards's letter to his friends and my inquiries into it introduce the issues and some of the terms that are central to this book.

> We in this town, were the last Lord's Day the spectators, and many of us the subjects, of one of the most amazing instances of divine preservation, that perhaps was ever known in the land. Our meeting-house is old and decayed. . . . It has been observed of late that [it] has generally spread at the bottom; the cells and walls giving way, especially in the foreside, by reason of the weight of timber at the top, pressing on the braces that are inserted into the posts and beams of the house. It has done so more than ordinarily this spring; which seems to have been occasioned by the heaving of the spring thaws. By this means, the under-pinning has been considerably disordered; which people were not sensible of till the ends of the joists which bore up the front gallery, were drawn off from the girts on which they rested by the walls giving way. So in the midst of the public exercise in the forenoon, soon after the beginning of the sermon, the whole gallery—full of people, with all the seats and timber, suddenly and without any warning—sunk, and fell down with the most amazing noise upon the heads of those that sat under, to the astonishment of the congregation. The house was filled with dolorous shrieking and crying; and nothing else was expected than to find many people dead, and dashed to pieces.
>
> The gallery in falling seemed to break and sink first in the middle; so that those who were upon it were thrown together in heaps

before the front door. But the whole was so sudden, that many of those who fell, knew nothing at the time what it was that had befallen them. Others in the congregation thought it had been an amazing clap of thunder. The falling gallery seemed to be broken all to pieces before it got down; so that some who fell with it, as well as those who were under, were buried in ruins; and were pressed under heavy loads of timber, and could do nothing to help themselves.

So mysteriously and wonderfully did it come to pass, that every life was preserved; and though many were greatly bruised, and their flesh torn, yet there is not, as I can understand, one bone broken or so much as put out of joint among them all. Some who were thought to be almost dead at first were greatly recovered; and but one young woman seems to remain in dangerous circumstances . . . but of late there appears more hope for her recovery.

None can give account, or conceive, by what means people's lives and limbs should be thus preserved, when so great a multitude were thus imminently exposed. . . . It seems unreasonable to ascribe it to any thing else but the care of Providence, in disposing the motions of every piece of timber, and the precise place of safety where every one should sit, and fall, when none were in any capacity to care for their own preservation. . . .

Such an event may be sufficient argument of a divine Providence over the lives of men.[1]

The editors of Edwards's works indicate that the collapse might be seen "by the unthinking world to be a signal token of God's displeasure against the town." Instead, because of the conversion of many persons it is seen to be a token of God's goodness.

Edwards, the enlightened observer of the physics of buildings, provides a thoroughly naturalistic—scientific—description and explanation of the collapse of the gallery. Edwards, the Reformed pastor and theologian, provides a theological description and explanation, or at least interpretation, of the same event and its outcomes.

Does Edwards give us two different *descriptions* of the same event—one of the timbers falling, and the other of providential activity? Does he give us two different *explanations* of the same event—one a naturalistic causal explanation of frost heaving to make unsteady a building already with noticeable structural problems, and the other a theological explanation of a divine providential intention? Does the naturalistic explanation *necessitate* the particular theological one that is given? Does it limit possible theological interpretations?

The editors indicate that the "unthinking world" might assume that the collapse is "a signal token of God's displeasure against the town." Why is Edwards's theological account correct, and that of the "unthinking world" incorrect? Are the same event and the same naturalistic, physical explanation of it susceptible to two radically different theological interpretations?

If that is the case, does it mean that a theological explanation is not *determined* in any way by a physical explanation of the same event? Was it the outcomes of the event—no one killed and many conversions—that provided sufficient evidence for Edwards's providential theological explanation? What if there had been many killed and a significant apostasy as a result? Then would the unthinking world's explanation have been theologically correct? Would many deaths and apostasy have counted against a providential explanation? Or could one simply give a different providential account? For example, that God collapsed the building to warn the congregation and the town of Northampton that they ought to repent. Or could another pastor or theologian interpret the event to be a sign of God's wrath and judgment, not God's providence? Can *any* and *every* description and explanation of any and every event also be given a providential description and explanation? Does the physical account in any way determine—limit or license—the religious and theological account? the interpretation of divine action?

Or are the two descriptions and explanations different because Edwards moves from one framework of *evaluation* to another? The scientific, physical, external observer's account values objective, verifiable information and scientific principles of explanation. The theological account values the religious significance of what has occurred. Are these two frameworks of evaluation incommensurate with each other, like two radically different "language games" used to narrate the same event?

Or does Edwards, the pastor and theologian, look for a religious *meaning* in the processes and outcomes of an event that can be scientifically explained? If so, does the scientific explanation in any way control—license or limit—the possible religious meanings? Could some other pastor or theologian from a non-Reformed tradition find a radically different religious meaning from Edwards's? Or might Edwards, on another day, have found a different religious meaning?

A passage from Calvin's *Institutes* describes, explains, values, and gives religious meaning to another physical event, a biological process. I shall only quote it, and not comment on it. It serves as another illustration of issues central to this book, to which I shall occasionally recur.

In a section of book 1, headed "God's providence governs all," Calvin cited Psalm 8.

> David exclaims that infants still nursing at their mothers' breasts are
> eloquent enough to celebrate God's glory, for immediately on coming
> forth from the womb, they find food prepared for them by his heavenly

care. Indeed, this is in general true, provided what experience plainly demonstrates does not escape our eyes and senses, that some mothers have full and abundant breasts, but others' are almost dry, *as God wills to feed one more liberally, but another more meagerly.*[2]

These illustrations might seem archaic, coming as they do from the eighteenth and the sixteenth centuries, respectively. One might think that Edwards and Calvin are naïve, or that our sophisticated contemporary theological, pastoral, and moral activity has long since made their views outmoded.

Other illustrations are possible. Written texts, as well as actions and events, are addressed and accounted for by different disciplines, including theology. Not only theologians and preachers, but historians and literary scholars have addressed biblical texts for several centuries. How the incoming traffic from literary and historical disciplines, perspectives, methods, and interests is to be directed by scholars and preachers who are concerned about theology and the religious meaning of the texts continues to be a matter of controversy and discussion. Theologians and preachers have to determine whether and how other kinds of scholarship affect what they write and say. Most theologians have accommodated the traffic from historical and literary disciplines; many have addressed the problems involved directly, methodologically; others have addressed them obliquely; and still others are adept at finding ways to avoid the snarls. Arguments, such as Van Harvey's in *The Historian and the Believer,* cannot easily be dismissed.[3] The outcomes of the current Jesus Seminar are critically responded to by scholars who defend a theological interpretation. Major proposals for the resolution of the issues, such as Hans Frei's *The Eclipse of Biblical Narrative,* acceptably untangle the most difficult snarls of some theologians.[4] Traffic from historical- and literary-critical studies of Scripture continues to cross into theological studies, and proposals to make a smooth flow continue in scores of books and articles published annually. The various quests for the historical Jesus, for example, all grapple with the fundamental question of whether conclusions from historical and literary scholarship should, or should not, determine or qualify his theological and religious significance for Christians. I shall not analyze the Bible as the locus of intersections of disciplines, but call attention to it as another illustration of significant matters for the Christian churches that could be analyzed from the agenda of this book.

It is important to note that the issue of how different disciplines cross many intersections in research and writing, public affairs and events, and thus affect their interpretations, is not unique to religion and theology. It pervades academic research and teaching all across university life, and also public discourse. The same actions, events, and texts are intersections of scholarship that are addressed and accounted for from different disciplinary directions throughout scholarly work. Indeed, much of academic publication and discourse in lectures and seminars centers on negotiations between alternative descriptions, explanations, and other kinds of interpretation of the same subject matter. The potlatch ceremony of the Native Americans in the northwest part of our continent is explained and interpreted differently by a cultural anthropologist and an economist. Human actions are interpreted differently by a Kantian moral philosopher, a Freudian psychoanalyst, a neuroscientist who is an eliminative materialist, a social determinist, a Marxist, and a rational choice theorist. Causes of the same historical event, for example, the Second World War, are explained differently by a diplomatic historian, an analyst of political behavior, and a scholar who studies individual leadership. The issues for theology and religious discourse are distinctive, but not unique.

It is axiomatic for this book that how naturalistic and scientific accounts are related to theological, pastoral, and moral activity continues to be a critical matter in religious discourse: not only in abstract discussions about the relations of physics or biology to the doctrine of God, or of scientific to theological methodology—the locus of much of the science and religion or science and theology literature—but in systematic theology, moral theology, preaching, pastoral care, and choices made about social, interpersonal, and other relations and actions. Every time a pastor responds to a person whose painful and terminal illness is explicable by evidences and theories from medical sciences, her words and care imply a position on a spectrum of how scientific accounts are, or are not, relevant to theological and religious interpretations of the same phenomenon. Every time a Christian just-war theorist addresses the political, historical, and military conditions of a particular international crisis, she has to decide whether and how various accounts of them qualify or are applied to her religious moral argument.

The primary *descriptive axiom* of this project is: the same actions, events, texts, and other phenomena that are addressed or accounted for by theological, ethical, moral, and other religious discourse are also addressed and accounted for by other academic disciplines, and vice versa. Actions, events, texts, and other phenomena are *intersections* in which theology and ethics and other academic disciplines meet: for example, the collapse of the gallery in Northampton and the process of lactation are intersections in which naturalistic, scientific accounts meet theological and other religious accounts. Edwards's and Calvin's religious beliefs require a theological interpretation of events that are explained naturalistically.

The primary *analytical inquiry* of this project is: What kind of traffic takes place between other disciplines on the one hand, and theology and ethics and other religious discourse on the other hand? Do they meld into a smooth current flowing in the same direction? Are there head-on collisions between then? Do they turn off sharply so each can avoid the other as they travel? What implicit or explicit justifications are used in *rejecting, absorbing, and being determined by, or accommodating* evidences and theories from other disciplines in religious discourse? Can activity in the intersections be analyzed, compared, and evaluated?

The *normative question* is: What criteria ought theology, ethics, and other religious discourse use in rejecting, absorbing, or accommodating information and theories from nontheological disciplines and discourse?

I shall not examine the issues primarily at an abstract epistemological level, as much of the literature on science and theology does, but always keep in mind some denser, recalcitrant "thick" descriptions, like a collapsing gallery and breast-feeding. To borrow a metaphor used by the comparative mythologist Wendy Doniger, in my examination of the issues I do not use a telescope, but I do occasionally use a microscope.

When the same actions, events, texts, and other phenomena are addressed or accounted for by both scientific or other nontheological disciplines on the one hand, and theology, ethics, and other kinds of religious discourse on the other hand, how do nonreligious accounts *affect* the theological or religious ones? The ideal-typical options are limited. (The ideal-typical, or constructive typological, procedure I employ is meant to differentiate between distinguishable "types" of responses. The typology and its individual types are heuristic devices to aid understanding of particular differences of interpretations, and to make comparisons between them.)

1. Reject: religious discourse can account for any event that, for example, historians or physicists account for, as the religious writer chooses, since the two kinds of discourse are *incommensurable*. From this stance—a rejection of any theological or religious significance of information and theories from nontheological disciplines—one can have double or quadruple truths. Thus Edwards could explain the collapse of the gallery naturalistically, but also as a sign of divine providence—two different "truthful" accounts of the same event. Or, more extremely, the only truth is the theological truth; a religious account can claim that the scientific account is false, as some biblical creationists claim evolutionary evidences and theories to be.

2. Absorb and be theologically *determined* by scientific theories and information: This is the other extreme: an account by a biologist, physicist, or psychologist determines the theological or religious significance of the same event or action. An example is when an evolutionary theorist who has interest in theology deduces from the evidences and theories of physics, geology, and biology that God is the indwelling (immanent) ordering power of nature. Calvin's observation of differences in lactation determines his religious and theological interpretation of them, *given* his account of how divine intentionality is related to secondary causes. The indisputable biological fact that some mothers have full breasts and others insufficient milk determines his theological conclusion, that is, that God wills to feed one child more meagerly and another more liberally.

3. Accommodate: between the extremes there are many possibilities. This

ideal-type illumines the positions of most Catholic and Protestant academic theologians, and most educated Christians. A scientific or other nonreligious account *limits but does not determine* the possible religious accounts. It determines what cannot be included in a religious account, but does not limit what can be included. Or, the nonreligious account *authorizes but does not determine* the theological or religious account. The scientific account justifies a fundamental direction of a religious account, but it does not exhaust it. There is a claim for varying degrees of compatibility between the scientific and the theological accounts. My recollection of Jürgen Moltmann's theology is that he found a happy compatibility between scientific cosmologists' interpretations of an expanding universe and his doctrine of God, which supports a theology of hope. Does scientific cosmology authorize but not determine his doctrine of God? Or, is scientific cosmology a confirmation of the doctrine of God? Or is there simply a serendipitous concurrence between the two?

F. D. Maurice described some of his writings as "digging and spading," and so far this introduction has been doing just that. I have introduced the essential subject matter with the extended illustration from Edwards and the briefer one from Calvin, and I have introduced terms and distinctions that will be developed and used throughout the book.

The Importance of This Project

Why is this project an important one for theology, ethics, and religious leadership? First, the Warfield Lectures from which the first five chapters derive were by stipulation to attend to the Reformed tradition in theology. But my claim is that the agenda is equally applicable to other theological and religious traditions as well. A comprehensive treatise could take up the issues in all religious traditions, not only Christian. For any heirs of the Reformed tradition (my primary example), whether by birthright or adoption, if they respect at all its primary generating source, the subject matter of this book is absolutely unavoidable. In sections headed "Understanding as regards art and science," and "Science as God's gift," Calvin wrote that capacities for art and the sciences are "bestowed indiscriminately upon pious and impious"; they are "rightly counted among natural gifts." Further, "Whenever we come upon these matters in secular writers, let the admirable light of truth shining in them teach us that the mind of man, though fallen and perverted from its wholeness, is nevertheless clothed and ornamented with God's excellent gifts. If we regard the Spirit of God as the sole foundation of truth, we shall neither reject the truth itself, nor despise it wherever it shall appear, unless we dishonor the Spirit of God."

"Shall we say," he continues, "that the philosophers were blind in their fine observation and artful description of nature? Shall we say that those men were devoid of understanding who conceived the art of disputation and taught us to speak reasonably? Shall we say that they are insane who developed medicine, devoting their labor to our benefit? What shall we say of all the mathematical sciences? Shall we consider them the ravings of madmen? No. . . . We marvel at them because we are compelled to recognize how preeminent they are."[5]

Note where this passage comes from: book 2 of the *Institutes*, "Knowledge of God the Redeemer in Christ." In the midst of a book focused on how saving knowledge of God comes only through biblical revelation and preeminently through Christ, Calvin reiterates themes found in book 1, "Knowledge of God the Creator." The truth about nature, derived from the sciences, has its foundation in the Spirit of God. Surely, then, that truth intersects with theological interpretations of nature, events, and actions. Therein lies our subject.

One would have to be a traditionalist if passages such as these were sufficient to claim the importance of this project. Because Calvin wrote those words is not a sufficient reason to pursue, centuries later, some inferences than can be drawn from them about other disciplines in relation to theology. Calvin, Thomas Aquinas, and many other persons in the Christian tradition, going back at least to Justin Martyr (second century), recognized that biblical theology had to be supplemented by other sources of knowledge to develop an adequate theological interpretation of nature, events, and actions. Theology, ethics, and other forms of religious discourse have seldom, if ever, been done in an intellectual or cultural vacuum. This project is not novel. It is in line with a great tradition. This tradition is significant not because it is tradition, but because major authors saw the intellectual necessity of taking into their accounts the realities that secular sciences and philosophers accounted for naturalistically.

Second, this project, as I previously claimed, is important for the work of ministry: preaching, pastoral care, and moral action. Everyone—not only the highly educated—in our culture confronts scientific, economic, psychological, political, and other nonreligious, nontheological descriptions and explanations of actions, events, and other phenomena. Everyone is exposed to multiple interpretations in daily papers and news magazines, in movies and on television—for example, *Nova*—and in other media. I know of few persons who use religious and theological symbols, concepts, and language as their first order of language to interpret themselves, their relationships, their health and illness, their work and leisure, or economic and political events, and so on, that occupy their attention. Even when professional users of religious discourse—theologians, teachers, or pastors—speak about political, economic, or social events they first use the language of politics, economics, and sociology, or the common language of news-speak. They never, in my limited experience, use biblical or religious language. Personal crises are spoken about in psychological or social terms more than in the language of sin, judgment, redemption, and regeneration. Pain and illness are accounted for in medical terms, and family catastrophes are viewed in complex social terms, rather than as evidences of divine sovereignty.

Every person who, in the face of severe pain, life-threatening illness, or other catastrophes, asks, "Why is God inflicting this on me?" is raising the central issue of this book. That is, what is the relation between the naturalistic or scientific description and explanation of an event on the one hand, and a religious interpretation of it—its meaning, for example—on the other hand? Every pastor, counselor, or friend who answers that question is making a judgment about the subject matter and issues of this book.

Bible-speak or theological terminology is not the first language of anyone, including biblical theologians, with whom I have ever conversed. George Lindbeck's commendation of "the ancient practice of absorbing the universe into the biblical world" does not come naturally to anyone I know.[6] It is hard to determine what *the* biblical world is; there clearly are many. Even if one could, it is not easy to *absorb* neuroscience and genetics, black holes and quarks, viruses and broken limbs, Alzheimer's disease and bipolar disorder, Palestinian–Israeli and Northern Ireland tensions into biblical, theological, or other religious discourse. Theologians, pastors, and everyone else now live in a culture in which we are daily exposed to alternative accounts of the same actions, events, and other phenomena—that is, we live in a culture that evokes what for decades was called "cognitive dissonance."

One can only guess whether and how much this cognitive dissonance between the language of nontheological disciplines and theological and religious discourse used in preaching and pastoral activity poses spiritual, moral, and theological quandaries in the minds of participants in church life. For at least some it does. It is surely a cause of disaffection from Christian churches on the part of many persons, both young and old. They find secular accounts to be sufficient. This project is important pastorally insofar as both clergy and other participants in church life confront and are concerned about the dissonance between naturalistic explanations of actions and their religious significance or insignificance.

Third, this project is important for theological scholarship and teaching. To be sure, after decades of neglect by most Protestant theologians, except those gathered around the Unitarian Ralph Wendell Burhoe, and the journal *Zygon*, science and religion, and science and theology, have become topics of almost faddish interest. This is fueled by the largesse of the Templeton resources. These resources are (in my observation) ideologically driven in that they support only teaching and research programs that issue in some reduction of dissonance between science and religion.[7]

The descriptive axiom of this project asserts the necessity for careful examination of places in which intellectual traffic from theology and religion flows from one direction, and "science" as a single cultural phenomenon and specific sciences from other directions. I remind you of that axiom: the same actions, events, texts, and other phenomena that are addressed or accounted for by theological, ethical, and other religious discourse are also addressed and accounted for by other academic disciplines, and vice versa.

One inference I draw from this is that theology and ethics, like other university disciplines, do not have complete autonomy; they cannot self-legislate their subject matter and its methods insofar as subjects they address are also addressed by other disciplines. What one sees across university research and teaching—namely, that boundaries between traditional disciplines become more and more porous because the subjects studied cannot be exhausted by one approach—is no less the case between theology and ethics on the one hand, and physical sciences, social sciences, and secular humanistic research on the other hand. And it is the trajectory of this project that just as some historians modify their studies after a serious encounter with anthropology, or literary scholars alter their interpretations after studying Marx or Freud or Nietzsche, or biologists reshape their work after studying physics and begin to do biophysics, so also those who work in theology and ethics have, at least, to reconsider their subjects and methods in response to other disciplines that intersect them. As I stated earlier, the negotiations between, for example, economics and anthropology over the best explanation of the potlatch ceremony are detailed and vigorous; so also negotiations between, on the one hand, theology and ethics and, on the other hand, research from other disciplines that intersect them have to be detailed and vigorous.

Theology and ethics have no privileged academic independence. Even if theologians lay claim to a unique, and thus privileged, source of knowledge in the biblical witness, their work intersects with interpretations of other disciplines at many points. Indeed, biblical narratives and other biblical discourse are religious and theological interpretations of nature, actions, events, and other phenomena that are describable and explainable in nonreligious language and concepts. Creation narratives are about nature: water, air, earth, animals, and humans. Exodus narratives are about an oppressed minority, migration, and contacts between diverse cultures. Legal texts are about sexual behavior, economics, and torts. Historical narratives are about territorial rights, military power, and warfare. Prophetic discourse is about interreligious and cross-cultural conflicts, relations between nations, and apostasy from moral and religious traditions. Eschatological discourse is about prognostications of future events. Salvation discourse, as recent apologists like to say, is about wholeness and health; it is about release from guilt. Since biblical times, theologians have continued to address or account for the same realities and experiences.

Only if theologians claim complete autonomy, or claim the incommensurability between religious and theological discourse and other forms of academic discourse, could they, even in principle, escape the issues of these lectures. Such theologians would have to defend the notion that their work is incorrigible from the point of view of any other discipline and, in effect, that it is intelligible only from within its privileged position.

Of course, theologians as well as parish ministers, either self-consciously or implicitly, have responded at least selectively to the agenda of this book. One thinks of F. D. E. Schleiermacher's rethinking of theology two centuries ago, among other things, of his interpretation of divine causality within and through natural causality as that was understood scientifically and philosophically in his time, and his consequent rejection of anthropomorphic views of divine will and intellect. The biblical view of God as person with an intellect and will like a human intellect and will requires revision in the light of the sciences. One thinks of Ernst Troeltsch's articulate confrontation with "modernity" in the early twentieth century: the implications of historical relativism, nourished for decades before in biblical and other scholarship, for traditional claims of the finality and exclusivity of Christian revelation; the similar implications of modern *Religionswissenschaft* with its scholarly studies of non-Christian religions; and the implications of modern scientific interpretations of nature as propounded by the physics and biology of his time. Only the most biblical literalists among pastors and preachers have not altered their interpretations of the Genesis creation narratives in the light of physical cosmologies and evolutionary geology and biology. Few, however, have altered their interpretations of eschatology in light of plausible cosmological accounts of the future demise of our species and the planet on which it developed. The practical query of these lectures is this: Are we sufficiently and critically conscious of how secular disciplines affect theology, and in turn affect preaching, pastoral care, and moral action?

Fourth, this project is important for ethics, both religious or theological, and secular. Every ethical theory, religious or secular, rests on a description and explanation of human nature and action. Augustinian ethics is philosophically shaped by the neoplatonic view of the human as directed toward ends by its desires, or loves, as is also the basic morphology of Thomistic ethics. Kantian-inspired ethics are based on the postulate that humans are radically free and have a capacity to govern their wills by deductive reasoning from the first principles of morality. Alan Gewirth's *Reason and Morality* argues that humans are voluntary and purposive—a combination of Kant and Aristotle; this descriptive premise is the fundamental basis of his normative ethical theory.[8] Utilitarian ethics are based on a description of humans as maximizers of what is pleasant and useful according to some structure of preferences. Virtue ethics, Christian or secular, either expound or imply a view of humans as having capacities for the formation of habits that can be shaped by action and oriented toward human fulfillment. Reinhold Niebuhr's influential political ethics were based on a biblical view of the human as sinners and retrieval of aspects of Augustine, the sixteenth-century reformers, and Kierkegaard. Schleiermacher's Christian ethics assumed that human participation in Christ's God-consciousness through the church would alter human activity; thus Christian ethics would be descriptive of how persons live in the kingdom of God. H. Richard Niebuhr's *cathecontic* ethics, the ethics of responsiveness and responsibility, find "man the answerer or responder" to be a better root metaphor of the human than "man the maker," or "man the obedient citizen."

Each of these views, and any other I can think of, claims some descriptive premises about the human to be more adequate than others. Each explains human action in ways consonant with these premises, and the prescribed, normative view of action developed by each is consonant with the explanation. Every "ought" interpretation of ethics is at least correlated with a description and explanation of the human "is." Each of these accounts is in principle susceptible to critical evaluation of its adequacy from the standpoints of current interpretations of the human coming from the human sciences—biological, psychological, or social.

The most persistent philosophical issue embedded in both religious and secular ethical theories has been freedom and determinism. All accounts of human accountability for action, and all prescriptive accounts of how human ought to act morally, assume a position on a continuum from complete determinism to the existentialist freedom defended, for example, by Sartre. Theological accounts of sin, as well as of the effects of redemption, when thought out in their ethical implications, can all be located at some point on the continuum. This persistent issue, in our time, requires a much more complicated response than the assertion of simple antinomies: determinism and freedom, or destiny and freedom—Tillich's favored terms. Various sciences describe and account for limits of human freedom, or, put in other terms, the extent of determinism. Moral philosophers and theologians might choose to ignore highly detailed studies of neurosciences and genetics that have implications for their descriptive premises about the human, and thus for their prescriptive moral theories, but they ought not to. The explanations of hate and love, of lust and power, that are given in synthetic accounts such as Melvin Konner's *The Tangled Wing: Biological Constraints on the Human Spirit*, or accounts of the social and cultural conditions that lead to high probabilities of violent behavior, and so on, have at least to be confronted and accounted for in some way in ethics.[9] Political science and other social sciences indicate the external constraints on human action, and the limitations that specific circumstances set on possible moral actions.

Ethical, like theological, scholarship addresses and accounts for the same events, actions, and other phenomena that nonreligious, nontheological scholarship from many scientific and humanistic disciplines also addresses and accounts for. Autonomy of the discipline of ethics is limited in similar ways to autonomy of theology. The issues of these lectures are as important for ethics, religious or secular, as they are for theology.

Strategies to Avoid the Issues

Of course, the fundamental and the particular issues of this book can be, and are, avoided by religious professionals—theologians, pastors, and teachers—in one or more ways. One way to avoid them is to confine the task of religious thought and life to the stimulation and nourishment of *spirituality*. I have in mind here many current emphases on spirituality, not the contemplation of God, the Ineffable, Unnamable, Indescribable beyond all comprehension that one finds in the Cappadocian fathers and others in the classic tradition. If the principal aim of religious thought and life is to provide ideas and conditions for individuals to achieve whatever experiences and senses of satisfaction are the aims of spirituality, then theology and other religious discourse are reduced to an instrumental, utilitarian function. Whatever theology, whatever religious discourse, whatever accounts of life in the world from the sciences or other sources are deemed useful to attain the outcome of some spiritually satisfying state are judged to be worthy if spiritual fulfillment is the aim of religious life and thought. The functional, utility value of religious ideas and activities justifies them. Their justification is not their truth, their defense on the basis of rigorous intellectual life, but the desirable outcomes for people who believe and practice them.

During a meeting about "spirituality and healing" a member of the audience contributed information, how accurate I do not know, from a study that there is now scientific evidence that prayer is beneficial to healing in a significant number of cases. I inquired whether this person knew if the experiments were controlled. What was the baseline from which, more or less, effects were measured? How was it determined that prayer was more effective than non-prayer? Was prayer more effective than favorite music? Was it more effective than hearing favorite poetry? Was it more effective than marijuana? If persons interested in spirituality are interested in the most effective mechanisms to achieve their desired states, prayer and religious beliefs can be compared for their efficiency to music, poetry, and marijuana. The question of their "truth" or intellectual adequacy can be avoided.

Whether there are defensible, intellectual, *theological* accounts of such efficacy of prayer or religious beliefs is in principle of no importance to many enthusiasts for spirituality. Also, major theological beliefs of the Christian tradition that must confront the issues of this book, such as the doctrine of creation, can be relegated to the background or avoided altogether if spirituality is the primary focus of religious belief and practice.

The main issue of these lectures, however, can be raised in an interesting way if spirituality is the dominant focus of religion. If spirituality is a state of consciousness, and if states of consciousness can be induced by physical

means—like my sherry each evening, or like breathing exercises that both In-
dian and Russian Orthodox mystical texts promote—one can inquire what the
relationship is between the physical explanation of the means to the religious or
theological account of the experience. Are these naturalistic explanations of
states of consciousness the secondary causes (to use one of Calvin's terms) of a
divine initiative, or the work of the Spirit? Or does a theologian or pastor give a
religious interpretation of the meaning of the naturalistic explanation? It is, of
course, one intention of these lectures to press questions like this on to view-
points that can readily avoid them.

Second, the issues of these lectures are avoided by some evangelical Christians who focus religious belief and practice exclusively on *individual, personal
salvation* from sin. The human condition of sin and its prescribed remedy are explained within limited biblical concepts and symbols. The ideational construction both for the self-interpretation of persons and for the prescription of
rectification can be hermetically enclosed from any naturalistic, external explanations or interpretations. "The Bible says" is sufficient authorization and explanation of the perilous human condition and of salvation from it. By a focus
of attention on individual salvation as the most important, if not sole, purpose
of Christian faith, life, and belief, other aspects of the tradition that cannot
avoid the issues of this book can be bypassed, such as nature as the theater of
God's glory (to borrow from Calvin).

Major theologians in the tradition, however, have given explanations of
human nature and action, and thus of sinfulness, that are not exclusively within
biblical constructions. One example is the Neoplatonic theological anthropology that explains human nature in terms of natural desires, or loves, of the good;
what Anders Nygren derided as the *eros* tradition. Both sinful and virtuous actions follow from desires or loves—sin from the wrong objects of love, or by having an excessive or deficient love for proper objects, in relation to God. Another
example is Reinhold Niebuhr's Kierkegaardian interpretation of a universal
state of anxiety that issues from our radical human freedom. Actions seek to
overcome that anxiety through idolatry, pride, and sloth rather than faith.

Whether these accounts of human nature, which are the bases for interpretations of sin, are adequate or "true" can be analyzed in light of various scientific accounts of the human. Insofar as a theological anthropology goes
beyond the confines of the biblical language and imagery in explaining the
human condition, it is susceptible to evaluation in light of alternative explanations of human nature and activity. Biological or social scientific accounts
might lead to outcomes that concur with traditional theological versions, or
they might require alteration of them. Various human sciences and philoso-
phies now describe and explain human behavior in the ways that Neoplatonic
or Kierkegaardian philosophy did for theologians.

It may be that the perplexing human situation that in evangelical Christianity is described as sin, and remedied by accepting Christ as personal savior,

is itself a construct foreign to many contemporary persons in modern cultures. For many persons, I believe that Paul Capetz's observation is the case: "From the Reformation to the Enlightenment there was a shift in the religious question itself from a concern with personal salvation from sin and guilt to a concern with the place and significance of human life within the comprehensive order of nature."[10] If this is the case, then the comprehensive issues of this book are more important now than previously. While some humans have always felt small and insignificant in response to the vastness of the skies and the countless stars, in contemporary cultures there are now more detailed explanations of the ordering of the physical universe, the emergence of the human, and of society than was the case only a half century ago. A preoccupation with salvation from sin and guilt may itself be a misreading of the human predicament as that is felt and understood by many people in our time. And its anthropocentric and individualistic focus may no longer be viable in light of interpretations of "the place and significance of human within the comprehensive order of nature" that are inferred from modern sciences.

A third way in which the issues can be avoided is by making theological and other religious discourse instrumental to *purely moral* ends, in personal and interpersonal morality, and in social morality. Whether religious beliefs, concepts, and practices can be defended intellectually is often not a concern of those for whom morally desirable outcomes are the chief purpose of theology and religion. Theology is in the service of ethics. Often, justifiable moral indignation in the face of forms of social oppression and injustice and their elimination, or at least mitigation, have been primary ends. Biblical or theological backings, such as exodus themes, are found to motivate and provide reasons for action. Theology and religious discourse are shaped by, used for, and justified by moral ends.

In interesting ways, nontheological disciplines are often the sources of descriptions and explanations of the circumstances that evoke moral indignation. For example, evidences of environmental deterioration and looming catastrophe, interpreted by theories about global warning, substantiate intuitive senses of alarm. The mounting of scientific accounts of present dangers and of prognoses of apocalyptic futures evokes moral and even religious responses. Respect or reverence for nature is elicited in the face of manifest evils that are scientifically described and explained, but induced by human activity and not by purely natural processes. Perhaps within or behind every environmental enthusiast is an inchoate sense of the sublime, a kind of religious sentiment and vision. This may be temporally and intellectually prior to forming moral and religious reasons for the deep concern.

Indeed, in at least some theological literature supporting environmental ethics, authors have searched *after the fact* for theological and religious backing of the social and moral concern. Some of the religious literature has accepted a historical argument that traditional Western Christian theology is the root of the problem—that is, its alleged biblical but anthropocentric view of all things being in the service of human. To recur to Capetz's observation, traditional Christian theologies of nature have to be changed in the light of scientific accounts of "the place and significance of human life within the comprehensive order of nature." To do this is not to avoid but to accept evidences from the sciences.

A fourth way of avoiding the issues of these lectures is more intellectually sophisticated; it is grounded in the fashionably facile view, *postmodern* in one form or another, that scientific, social scientific, and other accounts are social constructions of reality. They do not have sufficient validity to require any revision of religious, theological, or ethical discourse in their light. Religious apologists become philosophically adept at finding reasons to avoid challenges to traditional theology and ethics from various scientific and secular humanistic scholars.

Some of the current literature on science and theology or science and religion is more about epistemology than it is about either particular sciences or theological doctrines. It focuses on history and philosophy of science in relation to what I call philosophy of theology, that is, epistemological justifications for theology. Philosophers of theology are parallel in function to philosophers of science; some of them do not do theology and ethics any more than philosophers of science do biology or physics. In some cases, the weakening of the truth claims for science in general, or for particular scientific evidences and theories, is used to exempt religious thought from rigorous scientific criticism. I, however, cannot think of a plausible epistemology that would refute or relativize my opening illustrations, Edwards's and Calvin's accounts of natural phenomena—rather dense and particular accounts that required theological explanation as well. Observing that some mothers' breasts are full and others almost dry is hardly a social construction of reality.

Protestant theologians and church leaders who pronounce the death of "liberal theology," or labor to define a "postliberal theology," ought, in my judgment, to be more worried than they are about theology and religious life that ignore "the Enlightenment project." Their cliché, indeed mantra, dismisses liberalism. They are not always forthright about how much of the Enlightenment they have accepted, for example, scientific accounts of creation, or historical-critical methods in biblical and theological scholarship, and religious pluralism. Once theology has been exempted from criticism or correction from other disciplines by sophisticated philosophical moves, it easily invites acceptance of my fifth way to avoid the issues.

An example of this fifth way is provided by the television preachers I watch. These prophetic preachers, as they call themselves, use biblical passages from Ezekiel, Revelation, and other places to confidently interpret the eschatological significance of current political events and scientific developments.

News reports are accepted uncritically, and their meaning is interpreted through the use of biblical passages. One preacher explained a catastrophic earthquake in the San Francisco Bay area by noting that large pro-abortion rallies had occurred in front of the San Francisco City Hall two days previously. There is no way in which evidences and theories from the sciences could ever mandate change in their use of biblical religious and theological language.

Many fundamentalists, of course, have become more intellectually sophisticated, partly in light of the "postmodern" relativization of scientific claims, and thus seek on rational grounds to refute the claims of evolutionary theories. Their efforts to refute arguments for cosmic, geological, and biological development are designed to reduce confidence in them, and thus open the window for their biblical imagery and explanations. There are, of course, disagreements among creation scientists over ways in which scientific accounts can be accommodated in their theologies; they are not all of one mind.

In this opening chapter I have done four things. First, the long quotation from Jonathan Edwards, and the briefer one from Calvin, illustrate events and processes that are given both naturalistic and theological interpretations by the same author: the collapse of the gallery in the meetinghouse in Northampton and lactation in mothers after the birth of a child. Second, I stated the large agenda of these lectures and briefly introduced some analytical distinctions that will be developed and used in subsequent chapters. Third, I showed the importance of the basic issues not only for theology and ethics as academic enterprises, but for preaching, pastoral care, and moral action. And fourth, I outlined some of the activities and procedures by which Christian religious leaders avoid the issues.

The Human

An Intersection of Disciplines

The first chapter introduced the inclusive project of this book. The two illustrations at its beginning, the collapse of the gallery in the Northampton meetinghouse while Jonathan Edwards preached, and John Calvin on lactation, indicate the specificity at which the analysis should be applied. A physical event and a biological process were described naturalistically and also described, explained, or interpreted theologically. The crucial descriptive axiom of the book cannot be lost from view: theology and ethics address and account for the same texts, actions, events, and other phenomena that other disciplines do. The analytic task follows: to examine the traffic that goes on in the intersections when different disciplines address the same subject, and more particularly how theologians and moralists relate their work to other accounts.

I introduced two sets of distinctions that will be adapted and used, although not always specifically referred to, in this and subsequent chapters. A typology of how traffic is directed in the intersections distinguishes between two extremes: one, the rejection by theology and ethics of any possible alteration on the basis of information and theories from other disciplines; the other, absorption of materials from other disciplines so that the theology and ethics are determined by them. Between these two are many forms of accommodation: other disciplines limit but do not determine theology and ethics, or (more positively) they authorize but do not determine all that is claimed by theology and ethics.

Another set of distinctions, cryptically introduced in the first chapter, will be referred to, when pertinent, as the book proceeds. Just as the potlatch ceremony of the Native Americans in the northwest sector of our continent is accounted for differently by an economist and a cultural anthropologist, so the collapse of a gallery is accounted for differently. In the collapse of the gallery, however, the two accounts are by the same person. The four processes I described flow back and forth among one another, but for heuristic purposes distinctions are useful. There are differences between *descriptions* of the same action, event, or other phenomenon. The economist describes the potlatch exchange differently from the cultural anthropologist. Edwards, the naturalist, describes the collapse differently from Edwards, the theologian. There are differences between *explanations*. An economist's arguments use different concepts and feature different information from the cultural anthropologist's. Edwards gave both a naturalistic and a theological explanation. There are differences in *valuation* or perspective: an economist's and a cultural anthropologist's perspectives differ in what each values as most significant. Edwards has two evaluative perspectives, that of an enlightened naturalist and that of a Reformed theologian and preacher. Differences occur in interpretation of the wider *meaning* of the event, relative to communities of interest. For the social scientists its meaning refers to academic debates about adequate scientific explanations, for Edwards the meaning refers to understanding the ways of God, and God's relations to the human.

The course of this book is important not only for the work of academic theology and ethics. It is also directed toward the work of ministry in its manifold activities of preaching, pastoral care, teaching, and moral action: self-consciously critical religious leadership cannot avoid the issues. And all religious persons have implicitly or explicitly accommodated between religious and secular discourse that has a common referent.

I referred briefly in the first chapter to *the human* as an intersection in which various sciences intersect with a basis for ethics, philosophical or theological. Also, theological interpretations of the human have to determine whether and how secular interpretations are to be taken into account. The most fundamental question I address now is this: *Can theological, ethical, and pastoral scholars claim complete autonomy for their interpretations of the human?* Can theological and ethical interpretations be self-sufficient? Or do scholars, teachers, and pastors alter or in other ways accommodate their interpretations in light of evidences and theories from various sciences and insights from humanistic scholarship? If they do, what and how do they select, and how do they justify their choices? My impression is that pastoral theology has incorporated theories and information from various human sciences, for example, psychology, more than systematic theology and ethics. To explore the human as an intersection, I shall set the context of the contested interpretations in our culture, and especially in university research and teaching, including theology, religious studies, and ethics.

Conversation about the Human

Human "nature" and *human activity* are addressed in one way or another in nearly every discipline in university life. The human probably rivals *nature* as the most general theme of scholarly inquiry and subject matter of teaching. It is an inter-section in intellectual, academic, cultural, *and* religious life into which traffic flows from the physical and biological sciences, the social and behavioral sci-ences, history, and all of the humanities. Human nature and activity are de-scribed, explained, and evaluated differently, and given different wider meanings by various disciplines, and within disciplines, including theology and ethics. A description of the dissonance among the many voices in the university makes clear that theology and ethics are not unique in the traffic snags, and that the task of determining the implications of various fields for theology and ethics is exceedingly complex. Yet substantially supported evidence and theo-ries from various sciences, as well as history and the humanities, cannot be ig-nored by scholars of theology and ethics. Indeed, theologians have rejected, or accepted, or accommodated in some way nontheological and nonethical schol-arship about the human and its place in nature and history.

Imagine a college student who, for whatever motive, is concerned to un-derstand human nature and activity. She has been nurtured in a Christian con-gregation, so she knows that humans are created in the image and likeness of God; that the rest of nature was created to serve humans; that God, like a per-son, issues commands that must be obeyed at the peril of adverse conse-quences; that God speaks to the prophets; that humans are sinners and accountable to God for their actions; that God forgives; that God loves each and every person; that the work of Christ makes all things new; and that when the kingdom of God comes there will be fulfillment of all things.

In her studies she enrolls in a liberating curriculum that exposes her to the richness and diversity of the sciences and the humanities. At some point she takes a course by a physicist who expounds a cosmology based on the big bang account of the beginning of the universe. She has to adjust her time frame to think in terms of billions and billions of years. In studying the theories of cos-mic and biological development she reads synthetic accounts by creative scien-tists. She learns that the chemical conditions for the most primitive kinds of life probably have not occurred in any other part of the universe, and if they have we do not yet know that. In a geology course she learns about plate tectonics and the separation of the continents, and about the fault lines that are still moving in the earth. She learns about the source of the strata exposed on a cliff side: the limestone, the different sandstones, the gypsum; and she learns that what is now a desert was once an ocean. She takes a field trip into a limestone quarry to see with her own eyes the fossils in different strata, or to Ghost Ranch in New Mexico to see the excavation of dinosaur bones. In a course in what used to be called physical anthropology, now called paleoanthropology, she follows the discoveries in East Africa that indicate humans evolved from ancestors they share with other primates. She might take particular interest in the work of scholars who, on the basis of DNA studies, seek to reconstruct human migra-tion from the point of origin across the whole planet. And, in a course in human genetics she learns that many of our genes are the same as those found in what was called "lower" forms of life, and that most of what we are genetically we have in common with chimpanzees.

Should she reject these descriptions, explanations, valuations, and meanings of the human in the light of her biblically based Christian beliefs? Or should she decide that these interpretations of the human are true, and therefore she should jettison her Christian ethical and religious outlooks and ideas? Or should her interpretation of the human accommodate itself to both these scientific accounts and her religious and moral outlook? Do they limit what she can say religiously and morally about the human? Do they provide information that authorizes her to formulate religious and moral convictions congruent with them and not discard her Christian beliefs?

If she is a receptive and reflective student, who studies first with a hermeneutic of appreciation rather than a hermeneutic of suspicion, she will describe the human in a much vaster scale of space and time than she would if she thought of the human primarily in interpersonal relations. Humans developed only after eons of time, and are an interdependent part of a hugely complex cosmic and ecological system. Unless she stands firm in a Western and Christian dogma that all things were created for the sake of the human—a point of view that can be amply found in biblical, Christian, and secular Western thought—she has to decenter the human, herself, her social groups, and her species. If the human, including herself, has emerged through eons of time, through impersonal forces of nature, through contingent natural events that could have been otherwise and had different outcomes, she must wonder whether one can continue to speak of creation by the Word of God, or the biblical imagery of God as person, personally related to each individual.

The context in which she and the human species are analyzed has changed. It is not a description of human actions as individual agents who make particular choices in specific circumstances, or of persons as members of an ethnic group or in intimate personal relations. Each and all are the outcome or effect of impersonal natural forces beyond her power to determine. The human is thus explained differently. Her science professors observe and study from a perspective that values the stance of the external observer, not the individual person who chooses and acts. She now knows *what* we are: the outcomes of impersonal natural powers. If this is the case, can the human have the same meaning it has for the biblical claim that we are created in the image and likeness of God? The biblical account seems to tell her *who* we are: persons who bear the likeness of God. But perhaps that biblical statement is a projection of some human characteristics on a deity, written before scientists could account for billions and billions of years of cosmic, physical, chemical, and biological development.

We will not follow our student through all of her courses, through the dissonance of voices from all the disciplines that address, or account for, the human. It is useful, however, to think about some of the other courses she has taken. She enrolls in a course in economics that focuses not primarily on institutions of finance and marketing but on human behavior. Human activities, even selection of a marriage partner and the birth and raising of children, are accounted for in probabilities, symbolized in calculus, which show that we are utility maximizers according to some ranking of preferences. She is given to understand that our activities can be explained without invoking our self-conscious intentions as reasons, or causes.[1] She entertains the possibility that even her own life as an active agent can be explained by inferences from her external behavior about what pleasure or other fulfilling ends she is maximizing. All of her activities can be explained: playing field hockey, working for a 4.0 grade point average, mastering the French language, partying, praying, going to religious services, or doing community service in a homeless shelter. She might have questions about this, based on a reading of a philosopher who distinguishes between acting, which is intentional, and behaving, which is not.

She finds concurring evidence for the economic description and explanation in courses in psychology, depending of whether the instructor is a strict Skinnerian behavioristic determinist, or a humanistic existential psychologist. Reading a book by a sociobiologist who projects from what is firmly verified about the genetic basis of behavior to implications of it for religion, ethics, and the human prospect for the future undergirds, at least temporarily, a conviction that human nature and activity are determined by causes susceptible to scientific explanations, if only in probabilities and not immutable laws.[2]

What happens to her understanding of the human when she takes a course in moral philosophy, and reads a textbook written under the powerful influence of Immanuel Kant? That textbook also is based on a description of the human, one that stresses the differentiation between humans and others, rather than the continuities and similarities. Humans are actors; they are free and rational, and thus can choose what runs counter to their natural desires. They can determine these choices and their consequent actions on the basis of deductive reasoning from the first principle of morality: respect for persons.[3] She wonders how the description of humans as radically free and rational, and a normative inference that action ought to, and therefore can, be determined by choice and not by maximizing some preferences, fit what she has studied in other courses. The moral philosopher seems to dismiss the sciences of the human as *explanations* of moral action; at best, for him those accounts interpret *conditions* for action, not *causes*. But maybe the moral philosopher is also maximizing utility according to a different set of tastes; what he invokes as justifying reasons for action may be only rationalizations for his order of preferences.

Our receptive and reflective student, with her Protestant Christian nurturing, is bound to wonder about how these alternative interpretations of the human relate to the claim that she is made in the image of God, among other Christian beliefs. She finds one way to manage the dissonance by reading Abraham Joshua Heschel's *Who Is Man?*[4] He states that explanations from biology, genetics, and other sciences cannot tell us *who* we are. They might describe *what* we are (not his term)—our similarities to other beings—but they cannot describe *who* we are. For that we can turn to reflection on personal experience and the biblical material. We have the capacity to be responsive to ourselves, to others, to the world around us, and ultimately to God. Responsiveness distinguishes the uniquely human, and it is our uniqueness, not our similarity with other beings, that gives the authentic description of our humanity. Nothing from sciences that stress continuity with all living things, or the social sciences that explain our behavior, can invalidate this interpretation of *who* we are. We are all bipedal mammals, and all products of our particular societies and cultures, but these only tell us what we are, not who.

Our student enrolls in a course in the Women's Studies Program. She learns about the many social restrictions, historically and socially, that have stifled women's aspirations, determined their self-understanding as subordinate to men, their remuneration, and almost every other aspect of their lives. She sees her upbringing in her middle-class Christian family to have inculcated these aspects of her own sense of who she is. Gender affects what we are as humans. Gender is a defining characteristic, socially constructed and not biologically determined, just as race is.

What can it mean as a woman, she asks herself, to be created in the image of God? What does it imply about God if a woman is created in God's image? Does the biblical image of God need to be revised in light of her womanhood? How do the evidences and theories about the distinctive features of women's moral experience—more relational and compassionate—affect her response to the Kantian moral philosopher? Is his rationalism based on some male characteristics? As she reads various books she discovers that feminists differ on important issues, for example, whether women should be described primarily in terms of how they differ from men and thus have special gifts and needs, or on the basis of a universal humanity they share with men, and thus claim a universal, radical equality with men. She may wonder whether the difference between feminist scholars is about the most accurate *description* of women, or about different *valuations*.

A course in Buddhism will make her wonder if there is a self, at all. Another course in religious studies, in modern Christian thought, will expose her to Reinhold Niebuhr's powerfully influential Christian interpretation of the human. She studies his tripartite analysis of body, mind, and spirit, and about the anxiety that human freedom creates. She learns his account of sin: humans are inevitably but not necessarily sinful. They overcome the anxiety of their freedom, of being spirit, by pride or by sloth. And both pride and sloth issue in destructive, indeed evil, outcomes. She pauses when she reads that it is "only" the Christian interpretation of the human that avoids the perverse errors of excessively optimistic and rationalistic views.[5] How, our receptive and reflective student might wonder, are these claims and outcomes related to the other descriptions and explanations she had studied?

This is an especially poignant question if she studies the comprehensive, synthetic account of the human by the biologically oriented anthropologist Melvin Konner, *The Tangled Wing: Biological Constraints on the Human Spirit.*[6] On the basis of many scientific studies, he has a view of the human that is just as realistic about evil as that of a theologian. But his explanation is entirely different from the theologian's. It is based on a synthesis of biological and other sciences of the human and on secular literature, not on the insights and truths of the Bible, Augustine, Luther, and Kierkegaard. Of course, she quickly notes that the antidote to the human condition described by the theologian is faith and love, and to the scientist it is more and better research permeated by a sense of wonder.

Her instructor in Christian thought and ethics might defensively argue that the descriptions and explanations she has encountered in the biological and behavioral sciences are "reductionistic." He may even tell her that she is naïve about science. Scientific knowledge does not have the comprehensive truth and finality that she thinks it has. His is a common ploy, especially in some courses on religion and science. These sciences cannot describe what is uniquely human, nor can they individually or collectively fully explain human action. To this, if she is aggressive, she might respond that theology and ethics cannot explain what she has learned from the sciences. The instructor, however, specifies and develops his indictment in several ways.

First, he reiterates Heschel's point, namely, that the sciences can show only what humans have in common with the rest of the natural world. The Catholic tradition, however, has always accepted this in its interpretation of the natural law. Humans, like other animals, need nourishment and desire to procreate. Yet scientists cannot explain the *uniquely* human. In the natural law tradition the capacities for rationality, intentionality, and will are unique to our species. Her instructor offers this as one historical example; or he might argue that humans are spirit and not only flesh. Humans are self-transcending. Is Konner's subtitle not *Biological Constraints on the Human Spirit*? Is his "sense of wonder" a uniquely human quality that cannot be fully accounted for by the sciences?

She retorts that these claims for uniqueness, or at least distinctiveness, are dependent on, if not caused by, physical, chemical, biological developments and processes. Konner claims this. She points out the minuscule chromosomal differentiation between humans and chimpanzees as evidence that the sciences can explain the uniquely human. She cites the progress of neurosciences in accounting for differences between humans and other animals on the basis of different evolutionary developments.

Second, her instructor develops a slightly different indictment. In recent decades some historians and philosophers have argued that science is relative to special economic and political interests, that it is male dominated, and that its work is determined by concentrations of entrenched powers of governments and industry. The trenchant critiques of science and its culture by various "postmodern" writers are particularly persuasive. Sciences are not disinterested and universal; they are historically relative, not completely different from creative fiction. Thus their truth claims have been exaggerated. They do not deserve the credence that she is giving them in her interpretation of the human.

In a course in the sociology of knowledge she learned that all knowledge is relative to the social location of its producers, and thus relative to their time in history, their cultures, their intellectual interests, their resources, and their research methods. There has been a sociology of knowledge for decades, including scientific, theological, and ethical "knowledge." It occurs to her that in theology courses she has never heard of an Irish theologian who is a Lutheran, or a Swedish theologian who is not Lutheran. So, what's new about relativism? Her instructor's enthusiastic rhetoric will not have the effect he anticipated. She asks which particular information and explanations of the human he thinks are undercut by his general "postmodernist" critique of the sciences. Is he prepared to deny the evidences of the development of the human from ancestors common to us and other primates? To deny that Tay-Sachs disease is caused by one precise chromosomal abnormality? To dismiss a significant statistical probability that children raised in conditions of poverty and poor education are likely to engage in socially disruptive behavior? What other outcomes of research in particular sciences of the human is he prepared to dismiss, and on what basis?

Third, her instructor retorts that there are many continuing arguments between scientists about various aspects of human nature and activity. The "nature" versus "nurture" controversy continues. His colleagues in anthropology are divided among economic, symbolic interactionist, psychoanalytic, and biological perspectives. She counters that this is not novel, nor does it warrant a total skepticism about the sciences. Some of the arguments pertain only to specific evidences and their implications. Is he, she might ask, ready to substitute the Genesis account of the creation of humans for an account of its East African, or even earlier, origins? Indeed, she observes that he and most of his peers refer to the biblical creation narratives as theologically and morally meaningful myths, and do not claim that they are causal explanations. They have long made a decisive accommodation to scientific descriptions and explanations in this regard.

If so, are they using a "postmodernist" critique of "scientism" to justify credence for their theological interpretation? Does the fact that arguments continue among sciences of the human warrant skepticism about all the accounts she has read receptively? Does her instructor's "postmodernism" license him to deny any theological or ethical significance of evolutionary accounts? Does it license him to ascribe truth, but only mythic, nonreferential truth, to the Genesis accounts? Or, parallel to Jonathan Edwards, to affirm a naturalistic account—in this case biological and evolutionary—and also provide a theological interpretation of its meaning on scriptural bases? Or does he commend to her the cognitive dissonance between double truths about the same phenomenon?

She continues her interrogation of this instructor. Is he prepared to say that the fact that scientific knowledge is a human enterprise related to particular cultures and institutions, to gender and class biases, and can be shown to serve economic interests negate the Mendelian explanations of genetics on the basis of which Tay-Sachs and other genetically determined diseases are diagnosed? Is he prepared to deny the probabilities that statistical analysis can show significant correlations between various social and economic circumstances and behavior? Is he prepared to deny that hemophilia in descendants of Queen Victoria is not genetically determined? Indeed, does he not rely on the sciences whenever he consults a physician about symptoms of illness? If the sciences are said to be just a different "story," our student wants to know if that falsifies a lot of information her instructor apparently accepts.

Fourth, her instructor has yet another response. He acknowledges that the results of many of the human sciences cannot be refuted, and that, indeed, when he is ill and visits a physician, or when he thinks about limits of accountability for actions that mentally handicapped persons have, he accepts a biological explanation of it. Certainly he cannot disprove the results on scientific grounds. As a person of our time and culture with a good higher education, he is unwilling to substitute a literalistic biblicism for the scientific descriptions and explanations of many aspects of the human. He will admit that his religious and ethical thinking has made accommodations to scientific findings. But they have not subverted his theological perspective. Our student pursues him to learn how his accommodation works.

Would he say what Edwards said about the collapse of the gallery? Can he describe the human in scientific terms, and in the next breath describe it in religious and theological terms? Does he explain some human activity in terms of its biological or social processes, and then also explain it as God's acting and ordering? Does he echo Calvin on lactation, and say that what is scientifically described and explained is the expression of God's intention for a specific person or group of persons? If he does this, does he do it consistently? Does he say that the pain of metastasis, explicable in biological terms, is how God's purposes are being exercised? If he does not, how does he relate the sciences to his religious interpretation?

Her religion instructor, or some other instructor in the humanities, points out that as a *scholar*, she evaluates the human in one set of terms, namely, the external observer's causal explanation of human nature and activity. But, as a *person*, she cannot live without also valuing life in terms of its freedom, its unpredictability, its less explicable wonder and mystery. Yes, the scientific accounts are valid and reliable within the context of the purposes and methods of investigation. But the meaning of those accounts is not exhausted by that context. One has to consider their meaning with reference to religious questions. For example, what do they tell us about our experience of limits, our dependence on powers we do not create and cannot control? What do they tell us about the pain or joy we experience in our relations with one another, about our deep appreciation of natural beauty and our sense of loss when we see it destroyed, about our sense of guilt and remorse when we are unfaithful to our friends, about our moral responsibilities? Do the impersonal scientific accounts rule out a personal God who cares for each individual? Her religion instructor assures her that revelation, the biblical tradition, provides a sure and certain knowledge of God as person, indeed as a loving God. This leaves her in cognitive dissonance, with at least double truths, if not more, that are incompatible with one another.

Confronting Disciplinary Dissonance

Our student thinks she has shown her religion or ethics instructor to be unwilling to look in a wholeheartedly critical way at his interpretation of the human in light of the various sciences she has studied. But if she is a critical as well as an appreciative student, she will have to admit that the various sciences conflict with one another. There are different descriptions and explanations; the human is evaluated differently by various disciplines, and the context in which its meaning is interpreted varies. Behaviorist and Freudian psychologists argue with each other. She cannot reconcile the economist's description and explanation of the potlatch ceremony with that of Franz Boas, the cultural anthropologist. Of course, Gary Becker's explanation of economic activity as the maximization of a utility preference can be made to cohere with E. O. Wilson's expansive genetic determination of human nature. But can she make a rational choice theory of another economist or a political scientist cohere with a biologically determined utilitarianism? Perhaps, since the rational choice also maximizes utility. But doesn't rational choice presume something like what she read in her moral philosophy course, namely, that humans have a transcendental freedom and are not necessarily determined by inclinations? What does she do with a lecture by a famous anthropologist that indicts his field for the variety of perspectives and methods that are used, to the extent that he questions whether it is any longer a discipline?

She can force her instructor to face the question of how accounts of the human from various sciences relate to his theological and ethical interpretations, but she has to face the snarls in intellectual traffic that occur when various scientific accounts of human nature and activity differ from one another. How can she decide among conflicting interpretations on which she will rely in her own description, explanation, valuation, and meaning of the human?

How will she relate that to her Protestant Christian background: that the human is made in the image and likeness of God; that God has created and ordered all things to serve the highest of God's creation—humans; that God, like a person in authority, issues commands which must be obeyed; that humans are accountable to God for their actions; that God is a person who loves each individual, and who (like an indulgent parent—Calvin) forgives; and that there will be a fulfillment of life of all things in a life and a world to come?

Of course, our student's situation is no different from that of an academic theologian or moralist, a parish minister, or people in a congregation. All are exposed to some degree to dissonant interpretations of the human; all either reject the sciences, or choose to accept a scientific account and let it determine religious belief and practices even if the Christian tradition is revised or abandoned, or accommodate to evidences and theories from the sciences by selectively borrowing from them while also adhering to traditional Christian teachings.

Our student enrolls in humanities courses in addition to religion and ethics: literature and the arts, history, and philosophy. Her liberal education brings her into creative literature—drama, novels, and poetry, and into the arts—plastic, musical, and film. Can she read Euripides and Aeschylus, or Shakespeare and Strindberg, or George Eliot and Joseph Conrad, or Nadine Gordimer and Toni Morrison, or Mishima and Endo, or Mahfouz, or R. K. Narayan and Ha Shin, or John Milton and Wallace Stevens, without wondering about the sufficiency of the descriptions, explanations, valuations, and meanings of the human she has confronted in other courses? from more theoretically oriented scholarship, whether theology and philosophy or molecular genetics and psychology? Can she listen to a Gregorian chant, or concentrate on the Gospel text as she plays a CD of Bach's *St. Matthew Passion,* or listen to Benjamin Britten's *War Requiem* while contemplating photographs of the Coventry Cathedral without wondering whether neuroscientific research will ever be able to explain her deep response to them? Will one of the human sciences, or a combination of them, ever fully explain the creation of a bronze dancing Shiva she saw in a museum in Calcutta, or the great reclining Buddha in Bangkok, or Thorwaldsen's marble Jesus inviting worshipers to "Come unto me" in the Our Lady Cathedral in Copenhagen, or the Vietnam Memorial on the Mall in Washington? Will the sciences be able to explain how deeply moved she is by these works? Will psychological, economic, sociological, anthropological, biological, or even theological and ethical analysis ever immunize her from spiritual and moral vertigo as she walks through the Holocaust Museum in Washington, D.C.? Can accounts by historians, political scientists, and military experts of the Second World War, or the Vietnam War, allow her to view with equanimity the fear and the courage, the blood and gore of soldiers and sailors as they are graphically depicted in a war movie? Would they ever slow down her grandfather's racing heart as he watched a documentary film of the Battle of Myitkyina in Burma?

Like almost every college student in recent decades who studies contemporary American literature, she has read Toni Morrison's *Beloved*.[7] The story of the dreadful circumstances that shape the lives of slaves, of the striving for freedom and the courageous risks that are taken, of painful memories and the aspirations of those who have fled, and many more aspects of motivation, character, circumstances, plot, actions, and outcomes—these defy explanation by any of the particular theories she has learned. And it is not generalizations, but the densely detailed narratives that elicit empathy and affectively evoke in the reader the fear and the pain experienced by the characters, and the terror of the limitations of possibilities and ambiguities of choice. Even in the barest summary of the central action and event of the novel, Sethe's murder of her child, the reader confronts a description that defies simple explanation. Sethe, who has escaped across the Ohio River after giving birth to a daughter in the course of her flight, from where she lives in Cincinnati, sees her former owner and law officers coming to take her back into captivity. She murders Beloved, her infant daughter.

As she contemplates this murder, our receptive but critical student does thought experiments, turning to what she has learned from the sciences and from the humanities, including theology, to test the adequacy of some ideas. Was Sethe maximizing her utility according to a rank order of preferences? That might explain her act. She preferred her Beloved's death to the probability that the infant would be returned to Kentucky and grow up a slave. But then every action could be reduced to that explanation. That theory could not, however, explain or justify Sethe's preference, or "taste" as some economist might call it. Given certain assumptions, a behavioristic economic theory can account for any and every human activity. Was there a utility advantage to Sethe? Yes, according to her order of preferences. But what does an economic explanation omit?

Was the murder an act of freedom that could be rationally, morally justified? Slavery is certainly not a condition that respects persons in a Kantian sense. Could Sethe's respect for Beloved's person morally justify her murder? Is slavery so dehumanizing (note the normative use of the term here) that respect for the infant's humanity morally justifies killing her? Can murder ever be justified by respect for persons? Would this be similar to an event our student read about in the press: the driver of a lumber truck in Sweden was pinned into the burning cab after an accident. He asked his colleague, who had escaped, to kill him in order to avoid the suffering of immolation. Does compassion count as a justifiable reason for murder? Is compassion just an emotion that should be ruled by a rational deduction from a first principle of morality?

Maybe there was some genetic or evolutionary advantage to the human species as an outcome of the murder. Surely such would not be wholly sufficient either as an exhaustive explanation or even as a serious hypothesis. Even if there is a genetic basis for the protective act of the mother—protection that in this case required murder—one would be hard pressed to show precisely what the genetic basis was and how it determined the action. After all, there is a genetic basis for every human activity, including research in genetics.

Could an anthropologist who works with theories of symbolic interaction account for the murder? She might provide insight into some factors that were involved, such as the linguistic symbols that Sethe uses to express and interpret herself in the narrative and dialogue. But that could hardly provide an exhaustive causal explanation. The event could be disputed in the endless debates about whether culture and nurture are more determinative of human behavior than biology and nature. Even if the abstract polarity was used for a case study to argue the necessity of both perspectives, Morrison's narrative would still shock the reader.

Perhaps some scholar, or reader, who carefully reads the whole novel and reflects back on the murder would say that "in the light of" all that Morrison vividly depicts, whether it is directly related to the murder or not, the act is comprehensible, is understandable. This is hardly a causal explanation, and certainly not a monocausal theory. Nevertheless, the painful memories, not only of Sethe but of every major character, each of which the author depicts in vivid dialogue and narrative, as well as events, are sufficient at least to comprehend why Sethe would kill her child. The murder may be understandable, but is it morally justifiable? If for moral reasons the reader could not justify it, he could at least forgive it as an act done under psychological duress, or fear. It could not, he might say, have been a "free" action, and thus Sethe's moral culpability is limited.

Our student wonders if a theologian or pastor can provide a better account than the scientific ones. One could examine Sethe's action in the light of Jonathan Edwards's complex technical deliberations on "The Determination of the Will." Its theme is "that the will always is as the greatest apparent good is."[8] The apparent good is what is most agreeable to the mind. Edwards's discussion could provide one possible explanation of the murder, but it does not necessarily imply a moral justification of it. The cryptic phrase is carefully explicated philosophically; precise distinctions are made with John Locke always in the background. To focus on Edwards's discussion goes beyond what I wish to achieve in this book. It could, however, lead to an exploration of various theological accounts of freedom of the will, in comparison to scientific accounts of human action.

There is a commandment, "Thou shalt not murder." There are biblical and theological narratives and explanations that can be used to address the murder. It was not like David's arrangement to have the inconvenient Uriah die, since the "advantage" of Beloved's death to Sethe is in no way analogous to David's advantage. Would Nathan, who made David aware of the self-deception of his intentions, have condemned Sethe?

One or another interpretation of human sin might explain the murder. A moralistic interpretation would simply say that Sethe violated a command of God; thus it was a sinful act. Could it be classed as an act of self-defense, and thus be a morally justified killing? Traditional moral casuistry would say no. Was Sethe acting under duress? Sethe could have done otherwise than she did, and avoided the sin of murder. On further thought, though, she and her family would have to live in slavery as an outcome. She and others would suffer because she preserved her moral rectitude by obeying a divine commandment. Her culpability could not be excused on the basis that she was invincibly ignorant; the "facts" relevant to her choice were known to her.

Sin has its root and its fruits, Christian theology has always affirmed. A fundamental orientation away from love for God as the chief end and toward lesser loves leads to sinful acts, as the Augustinian Neoplatonic pattern depicts. Or failure to trust in God and trusting in what is less than God issue in sinful acts, as in Luther's view. Could a theologian work inductively from Sethe's murder of Beloved show that if Sethe had been oriented toward love for God, she would have acted otherwise under these threatening circumstances? Could a theologian say that the root fault was that Sethe did not trust in God, that her "God" in this case was familial self-interest, an idol? Would any theologian wish to say that Sethe was spirit as well as mind and body, and thus was anxious because she was free? Her murderous act, thus, could be explained as overcoming her anxiety, caused by her lack of faith.

These and other interpretations of sin could plausibly be used to describe, explain, evaluate, and provide a meaningful account of Sethe's action. But our Christian student would not find any of them to be more satisfactory than the idea of maximizing utility according to a preference. Theological accounts, if given epistemic privilege to describe, explain, value, and give meaning to actions, are as inadequate, indeed reductionistic, as other theories.

How might her pastor have dealt with Beloved? she wonders. She heard sermons before she went to college that echoed a famous sermon by Paul Tillich, "You Are Accepted." She recalls those sermons as she thinks of the murder of Beloved. Perhaps her pastor preached on the story in John 15, of the woman caught in an act of adultery, where Jesus suggests that whoever is without sin should cast the first stone. They all silently fade away. Who will dare to judge Sethe? Perhaps the pastor has, from his belief in the triumph of grace over law—which is what he understands Karl Barth's theology to say—assured his guilt-ridden parishioners that they can be freed by accepting the unconditional grace of God made known through Christ. Their sin, de jure, is forgiven. Their sins, whether abortion or lying or murder (?), are forgivable; they can de facto experience that in faith. They are accepted. Or recalling what he learned by reading Rudolf Bultmann, they have been "right-wised" with God. Their salvation has been earned by Christ, not by their moral rectitude. Could that take any of the tragedy, the suffering, the pain, out of Sethe's life and action?

Her pastor, in his pastoral care, has often confronted the destructive psychological and emotional effects of rigid Christian moralism, indeed, legalism. He might even have accused Roman Catholicism, with its numbering and grading of sins in order to be penitent, of being a destructive religious force, leading to—if he has read novels by certain Irish authors—mutilating guilt or deceitful hypocrisy. Nietzsche, he might think, was correct in his indictment of rigid Christian morality—it is a slavish morality. In his pastoral work, especially with women, he has seen the repressive effects of a Christian morality of self-denial. Our student concludes that her pastor would not harshly condemn Sethe's act. Indeed, as a counselor, he could explain it by what the narrative tells us of the abuses and deprivations of slavery. A compassionate and merciful interpretation of the novel would extenuate moral culpability for action. Her pastor understands before he judges. Would this abate the repulsion and the fascination that our student feels when she meditates on the death of Beloved?

Conclusion

This chapter is an extended, if somewhat cursory, account of how the same phenomenon, human nature and activity, is addressed by various disciplines, including theology, ethics, and religious studies. It is an example of the descriptive premise of this book. Do these different disciplines and fields describe the human in incomparable ways? Are their explanations mutually exclusive? Are they different because each values different human factors? If so, can the differences be adjudicated relative to their adequacy and comprehensiveness? Or does each have a different framework for assessing the meaning of human nature and activity? Different descriptions, explanations, evaluations, and meanings of the human are seen not only when religious thought is compared with secular thought. Religious thinkers differ among themselves, just as other humanists and scientists do.

By following our receptive, but critically reflective Christian student, I have intended to achieve several aims. One is to provide a narrative with which most, if not all, readers can identify, at least to some extent. Cognitive dissonance about the human might be more dramatic in a critical student than it is in one who earns high grades by agreeing with each course. Our critical student is anxious about the adequacy of her Christian beliefs and outlook because of the intensity of the intellectual confrontations.

Parenthetically, it is unfortunate that undergraduate curricula seldom, if ever, provide an academic milieu in which students can deliberate about the dissonance even within the human sciences and humanities, not to mention theology, and weigh the alternatives to which they are exposed. Also parenthetically, a para-curricular discussion of these matters that often took place in intellectually vital chapters of various student Christian movements seldom exists today. Exposure to the dissonance comes to laypersons, if not through their higher education, then through their television viewing, their reading of news magazines, and other media. It comes to clergy as well, and makes them conscious of contended accounts of the human in their own professional actions, and in the experiences and thoughts of their congregations. It comes to academic theologians and moralists, whose social roles require a greater critical self-consciousness of the points of contention, and of the processes by which the traffic from various disciplines is directed, especially as it converges with their theological and ethical teaching. It comes into theological education, in courses in theology, ethics, and pastoral care, where it is either confronted forthrightly, ignored, or in sophisticated ways bypassed.

Another aim, which requires more precise and technical attention than it has received in this chapter, is to alert readers to critical self-consciousness about the various interpretations of the human, and to consider wherein and why they differ. Left unexplored is how one would manage the incoming traffic from various routes of academic and communication media, that is, how one would adjudicate discrepancies; whether one can establish a smooth pattern of traffic, a complementarity among alternative accounts. This chapter is designed to address matters in specific, dense details (though not as specific and dense as desirable) more than in abstract discussions of epistemological conflicts.

The third and most significant aim is to raise questions I emphasized in the introduction to this chapter. I repeat them because of their perduring importance to the rest of this book. *Can theological, ethical, and pastoral scholars claim autonomy for their interpretations of the human?* That is, are their theological, ethical, and pastoral interpretations self-sufficient? Or do they change or in other ways accommodate their interpretation in light of secular sciences and humanities? I aver that they do. When they do, *what reasons do they give for their selections and usages?*

I reiterate my very simple ideal-typology of religious and theological responses to alternative interpretations: (1) *reject* them for some reasons—biblical authority, philosophical and historical critiques of science, and so on; (2) *accept* them and let them largely *determine* their theology and ethics; or (3) *accommodate* them to each other in some way. Two ideal-types of accommodation have been suggested: other disciplines *limit*, that is, rule out some theological and ethics interpretations, but do not completely determine what is said; and other disciplines *license* basic choices in theology and ethics, but do not completely determine what is claimed. Unless readers are biblical literalists, and thus claim autonomy and the self-sufficiency of biblical theology, or unless they believe that ethics and theology have to be inferred from current sciences, and thus surrender their independence, all are in the accommodation mode, one way or another.

The principal aim of this chapter, and of the following three, is pedagogical. It is to raise self-consciousness about what we do, and examine how we do it, why we do it, and how we justify our activity. Seriousness about these questions leads to a critical examination of some currently popular theological and ethical orientations, which I will argue against. The project of this book follows a classic liberal theological tradition: to see how Christian faith and life can be sustained and developed in interaction with the diversity of secular as well as religious life and thought in the contemporary world. Here I cannot dismiss "the Enlightenment project" as is currently done. Indeed, as an ideological slogan, that dismissal skirts the option of rejection. But in practice, even proclaimers of that mantra have made, and necessarily will always make, accommodations.

The agenda of this book, I dare to claim, is unavoidable in our time and culture by Christians—theologians, pastors, and laypeople. Whether the agenda will be addressed self-consciously and deliberately, or be answered haphazardly and unwittingly, is, to me, a passionately important topic.

Naturalistic and Theological

Interpretations of the Human

This chapter provides a more detailed and rigorous analysis of important theological interpretations of the human that are the agenda of this book.[1] But before focusing on the human again, I remind readers that the agenda is applicable to many more intersections than the human in which theology and ethics meet scholarly and popular traffic. The agenda is applicable to many other contexts; my focus on the human is only an extended illustration of what occurs in many other contexts. How do Christians relate current scientific cosmologies to the doctrine of creation? Should psychoanalytic explanations of guilt alter theological accounts? Or, a question to which answers have been given for more than a century: Are evolutionary interpretations of the cosmos and of life necessarily antithetical to a theological account of God's relation to nature? What do theologians, pastors, and others accept or reject from secular disciplines? How do they interpret the material? How do they justify their interpretations of it? Recall the descriptive axiom of this book: theology and ethics address or account for the same matters that secular disciplines do. The agenda is unavoidable, once awareness is raised.

In theology and theological ethics selection is made not only from secular disciplines, what is rejected or accepted or adapted, but also from the Bible and the Christian tradition. Why have I not heard sermons on many biblical narratives and other texts? In our daily biblical readings my wife and I go through whole books, unsanitized by lectionaries selected either by a committee or an individual according to some religious interest. An occasional preacher, I sometimes ponder how I would interpret a passage if I had to preach on it. I am often grateful that, unlike rabbis who expound a Torah portion for the day even if it grates on modern ears, I can avoid ethically and religiously embarrassing passages. What startles me is often the religious discourse of the Bible itself. It at least offends popular religious sentiments and certainly is not what I have heard on Sundays. For example, I think I have never heard a sermon preached on Psalm 58. "The wicked go astray from the womb. . . . O God, break the teeth in their mouths. . . . Let them be like the snail that dissolves into slime. . . . The righteous will rejoice when he sees the vengeance; he will bathe his feet in the blood of the wicked" (RSV). This is not the loving, forgiving, universally gracious work of God about whom I hear, whether it is based on sophisticated theologies of the primacy of grace, à la Karl Rahner or Karl Barth, a classical view of substitutionary atonement, or liberal Protestant sentimentality backed by current psychobabble.

We read the miracle stories in the Gospel of Mark. One does not have to have read David Hume anymore. In the twenty-first century scientific meteorological explanations of weather backed by satellite pictures of storms passing over oceans and continents come to mind when one reads that Jesus rebuked the wind and said to the sea, "Peace! Be still!" and the wind ceased and the sea became calm (Mark 4:35-41). The disciples, Mark says, were filled with awe, and well might they have been. A command by Jesus reversed the physical, meteorological sequence of natural events. This narrative is one about which many Christians opt to accept a scientific account; they let the science determine their response to the biblical account. It is not only an account of the authority and power of Jesus, but implies that natural processes, like the collapsing of the gallery in Northampton, could be reversed by a command. God, it implies, is not bound to natural causation. Only an imaginative allegorical interpretation or some claim to perceive a "deeper meaning" could eliminate the startling caesura to contemporary Americans.

If persons would avoid that account of a miracle on the basis of scientific meteorological accounts of weather, would they avoid other biblical or theological accounts on the basis of sciences, for example, the empty tomb in the resurrection narratives? I wish to sustain and further a critical self-consciousness about what is said and done where scientific and religious discourse intersect, not only by theologians and pastors, but also by laypersons in congregations. A passion that motivates this book is self-critical examination, bold forthrightness and honesty about our theological, moral, and pastoral claims and beliefs.

In my return to a focus on the human, I assume that most readers are in some mode of accommodation between one extreme of rejecting secular accounts as having no significance for theological, ethical, and religious accounts, and the other of letting the secular accounts determine what we can say religiously. In the remainder of this chapter, examples of how some modern theologians direct the traffic are analyzed.

Theologians on Sciences and the Human

1. Rejection-like Strategies

Secular accounts are rejected in several different manners. One, only noted briefly, is extreme fundamentalist interpretations of the Bible: its truth is literally representational. These interpretations continue. Wide current exposure to them comes from "Christian" television and radio: the Bible was dictated by God to the authors of its books; it is infallible on historical and natural matters and, indeed, no secular scholarship has been able to disprove the accuracy of any biblical accounts. The final argument is absurdly circular: the Bible authorizes its own infallibility. If this position is rejected by readers, whether theologians, pastors, or laypersons, they are in the thicket of the agenda of this book.

More interesting and important are the historically and philosophically learned treatises and sophisticated arguments that are designed to diminish, if not demolish, the authority of the sciences and other secular disciplines in order to free religious discourse from having to take seriously the substance and the agenda of this book. The critiques differ in the degree of specificity of the issues they address, the precision of philosophical or cultural analysis, and the radicality of their claims. And the critiques are shared widely in current academic discourse; indeed, the same authors, Foucault, Kuhn, Feyerabend, Derrida, Lakatos, Lyotard, and others, are cited almost as a litany of sacred names by critics who relativize scholarship in all fields, even physics and mathematics. The theological positions that share this general approach have been called "postliberal theology," "the new Yale theology," "unapologetic theology," "post-critical theology," and "radical orthodoxy." They share a similar critique of "modernity" but their theological outcomes are different.

The general tenor of this mode of rejection of secular learning, and especially the sciences, can be found in the description of a series of books entitled "Radical Traditions: Theology in a Postcritical Key," edited by Stanley Hauerwas of Duke University and Peter Ochs of the University of Virginia.[1] The series, it states, "cuts new lines of inquiry across a confused array of debates concerning the place of theology in modernity." "Charged with a rejuvenated confidence, spawned in part by the rediscovery of reason as inescapably tradition constituted," the authors return to scriptural traditions in order to retrieve "resources long ignored, depreciated, and in many cases ideologically suppressed by modern habits of thought." But no claim is made for the exclusive and final revelational authority of the Christian Scriptures and tradition. Indeed, the series invites Jewish, Christian, and Islamic theologians to recover and articulate "modes of scriptural reasoning as that which always underlies modernist reasoning and therefore has the capacity—and authority—to correct

it." "Unfettered by foundationalist preoccupations," the series calls for "a thinking and rationality that is more responsive than originative. By embracing a
postcritical posture, they are able to speak unapologetically out of the scriptural traditions." "Confidence in nonapologetic theological speech" is the hall-
mark of "Theology in a Postcritical Key."

A brief description of a series of books necessarily begs many questions.
The "posture" it announces, however, warrants some reflection on why it echoes
my type of rejection of secular disciplines as sources to be taken into account in
religious discourse. Scripture and tradition are, in this posture, on the offensive
against "modernity." The traffic moves confidently and swiftly from one direction, theology, to correct what comes from another direction, "modernist reasoning." Indeed, it claims that scriptural reasoning has not only the capacity,
but also the *authority* to correct "modernist reasoning."

The brief introduction to a series of books does not say what is included in
modernist reasoning. It no doubt includes the "confused array of debates about
the place of theology in modernity." I infer that among those debates are the impact of historical- and literary-critical studies of the Bible since it is now read
only as narrative; Schleiermacher's articulation of a theology that took account
of the philosophical and scientific interpretations of the world; Ernst
Troeltsch's careful examination of the implications for Christianity's claims to
be the final and exclusive revelation of God that come from historical and cultural relativism, the plurality of religious traditions, and the contemporary sciences; Tillich's, Bultmann's, and any other religious thought that takes seriously
"the Enlightenment project"—as the dismissive mantra often goes.

The posture of confidence is not based on the certitude that literalistic fundamentalism claims, what might possibly be called from the posture of this series, a kind of "foundationalism." Indeed, no claim seems to be made for a
revelational authority of the Christian Scriptures and tradition that would provide a *theological* warrant for the critiques of modernity. In this respect, the posture rings with the tolerance of modernity. One might judge that, given the
recognition that reasoning is from traditions (something not recently discov-
ered for the first time), the secular learning that claims truth-value is rela-
tivized. An implicit acceptance of the relational character of all knowledge
grants permission to analyze from scripture the world of secular scholarship
with a hermeneutic of suspicion.

Apparently, however, "scriptural reasoning" is not to be analyzed on the
basis of a hermeneutic of suspicion. One is startled to read "scriptural reasoning" in the singular. Is not the refined legal casuistry in the Covenant Code in
Exodus and the Priestly Code in Leviticus as much scriptural reasoning as narratives are? Reasoning by analogy, and so on? The use of "scriptural reasoning"
implies a canon within the canon, the parameters and perimeters of which are
undisclosed. Would all information and theories that might be used to criticize
and reform a religious tradition come under the presumably demolishing judg-

ment of being "foundationalist"? There is, in the description of the "posture," no warrant for traffic from sciences and other secular learning to engage the Scriptures critically, at least in three religious traditions. Neither the fundamentalist claim nor a Barthian claim that the Christian Scriptures have revelational authority is invoked by the "rejuvenated confidence" of this new generation of theologians and religious scholars. Just because it is "textual," a theological tradition is apparently incorrigible from modern secular learning. Does this assume that "Scripture" and "tradition" are coherent, if not monolithic realities, so no judgments need to be made among the diversity within them? Or about who is qualified to use them? Apart from the fact that the editors of the series are theologians, it would appear that a retrieval of the *Iliad* and *Odyssey*, the dramas of Euripides and Aeschylus, Platonic and Aristotelian texts, the Vedas, Puranas, the *Ramayana* and *Mahabharata*, Mithraic and Gnostic texts, Shakespeare and Goethe, and others, could also be warranted as sources for the critique of modernity. (The book I have read in the series uses Dostoyevsky.) Perhaps even the myths of the skinwalkers and other stories from Navajo and other Native American traditions might be legitimate—or maybe, since these are oral and not textual, they are ruled out.

Some of these theologians are critical of functional theories of religion as developed by social scientists. If my interpretation of the description of the aim of the series is not unfair, the justification for the series itself is functional. That is, religious traditions function as a basis for correcting confused debates about theology and modernity, and other aspects of modernist reasoning. That function, which in the discourse of postcritical theology cannot be "foundationalist," justifies the theological enterprise. There are no claims for the revealed truth, or even special validity and reliability, of scriptural and traditional texts. Indeed, somewhat ironically, *criticism* of modernity is the justification for theology in a *postcritical* key. If the capacity and authority to correct modern reasoning justify the use of religious texts, would not other texts that could critique modern reasoning with equal effectiveness have equal authority? It is only ironical, and not paradoxical, because theology is relieved from modernity's external criticism, and thus is "postcritical," in order to provide critical challenges to all aspects of modernity. The theologian reads everything with a hermeneutic of suspicion except her or his own scriptural tradition, and his or her own interpretation of it.

The most erudite and extensive critique of the significance of the social sciences for theology and ethics is John Milbank's *Theology and Social Theory: Beyond Secular Reasoning*.[2] The perspective from which the critical analysis of a vast amount of scholarly writing is made determines the critical analysis and the outcome. That perspective is similar to the "posture" of the series "Radical Traditions: Theology in a Postcritical Key." To engage in a detailed response to Milbank's interpretations of various social theorists, particularly sociologists of religion—Émile Durkheim, Max Weber, Peter Berger, and others—would require technical detail beyond the purpose of this book. Milbank's skill is to ferret out presuppositions that issue in excessively generalized explanatory theories of religion and other human activities—a not uncommon critique of reductionist assumptions that lead to reductionist conclusions. His hundreds of pages of critical philosophical exposition are in the service of his theological interests and conclusions. I quote one summary of them: "Theology can evade all and every social scientific suspicion, and history is its ally: written history, which produces exceptions to the supposed universal rule; lived history, which permits us always to enact the different. Ambitious social science—the positivist and dialectical traditions—belongs, in the last analysis, to the project of enlightenment: the challenge to the particularistic obscurantism in the name of the humanly universal. But this challenge is at an end, for . . . it was itself made in terms of metaphysics, and a 'religion.'"[3]

The polarities that Milbank highlights are reminiscent of the *Methodenstreit zwischen Naturwissenschaften und Geisteswissenschaften*, the methodological controversy a hundred years ago in Germany between the natural sciences and the sciences of the human spirit. The argument then, and now, is about the extent to which universal laws similar to those from physics can explain human nature and human action. Milbank, like others, invokes "the project of the Enlightenment" as the generating source for claims about the scientific laws. He uses the now familiar polarity of universality and particularity. (The contrasting terms in the *Methodenstreit* were nomothetic and ideographic scholarship.) Claims for universal principles or laws to explain anything human are themselves rooted in a particularistic philosophical and cultural tradition. Thus claims to universality are false, and are based on "foundationalist" metaphysical principles. "[H]uman interaction in all its variety can only be narrated, and not explained/understood after the manner of natural science." "So, while some scientific 'explanation' of segments of human behaviour remains possible, though precarious, this is never explanation of the human as such, or of human interaction as such."[4]

Milbank generalizes; he assumes that all the human sciences suffer from what has been called "physics envy." Indeed, Milbank's use of inverted commas around the word 'religion' suggests that the excessive claims function idolatrously. To be sure, there are books written by scientists of the human that aspire to what Milbank fulminates against. For example, some of these books extrapolate from the known about human genetics to explanations of religion, morality, and other human activity; one thinks of E. O. Wilson's *On Human Nature*. The "eliminative materialists" among the scholars of the relations of the brain to mental activity, such as the philosopher Paul M. Churchland and the biologist Patricia Smith Churchland, strive to explain all mental activity on the basis of biochemistry.[5] Or, as noted in the second chapter, some economists explain human behavior as a maximization of utility according to a structure of preferences. Durkheim did explain religion on the basis of its functions to provide social cohesion in a community. But most scientific studies of the human recognize multiple causes of human nature and activity, and state conclusions in probabilities, not universally valid laws.

Examples could be cited of excessive confidence in the explanatory capacities of various sciences to fully explain human nature and activity, and theologians, functioning as philosophers, have a right to be critical of them. Before two important questions are raised about blanket dismissals of the importance of secular accounts for religious discourse, the level or location of the intersection between theological and secular traffic must be noted.

It is not in thick and detailed reports of experiments that report factors that, at least partially, determine human behavior and actions, for example, genetic defects; social pathology traceable to economic, educational, and other severe deprivations; effects of family abuse or neglect, and so on. They meet on a very general and abstract map: where Interstates 20, 75, and 85 connect in Atlanta, not its clogged downtown streets; where Interstates 40 and 25 cross in Albuquerque, which one cannot find from our home address without a detailed map. The intersection is not in Edwards's account of a collapsing gallery, or in Calvin's account of lactation. It is in high-level debates about epistemology. If Milbank's position claims intellectual victory, any positive significance for theology from scientific and other secular accounts of the human is rendered dubious, if not dismissable. You are on the wrong interstate, and thus it is impossible to get to the right place. You thought you could get to US 30 without driving the streets from 57th and Woodlawn.[6]

Does a fundamental critique of the philosophical justifications of sciences of the human necessarily invalidate the significance of *particular* findings and explanations? Do, for example, Durkheim's or Marx's explanations of religion rule out that their accounts at least illumine, if not explain, many specific religious activities? A study of locations of burials, baptisms, and other rites correlates with the hierarchical class structure of Swedish society for many centuries. A significant geographical correlation during the late-nineteenth-century industrialization is drawn between different religious and political affiliations. Areas with many pietists and revivalists had fewer Marxists; those with many Marxists had fewer pietists. The hypothesis is that a proletariat was formed by persons uprooted from rural settings: many persons coped with the resultant anomie either in pietism and revivalism or in labor movements. (The politics of both my paternal and maternal families can be understood in part by this hypothesis.) The critiques of "modernist reasoning" address issues at the interstate intersections, or what I have elsewhere called the "star wars level." They do not examine particular scientific studies of the human, where information and interpretation address specific human actions and behavior.

Molecular biology is a "natural" science of the human, as are endocrinology and other specialized biological sciences. Molecular biological research is the basis on which predictions of probability of radical birth defects are made;

endocrinology and other research is the basis on which diagnoses of illness are made. Does the postcritical theological critique of modernist reasoning rule out the validity and reliability of this kind of research? Probably not. But does it eliminate these as causal factors that affect human action? If not, should it not acknowledge that it is part of "the Enlightenment project"? A chromosomal aberration causes Down's syndrome, which limits the mental capacities of the victims of this disease. Does a massive critique of the presuppositions of modernist scientific reasoning eliminate the necessity of examining carefully the relations between inherited physical conditions and human interaction? Is the account of self-destructive behavior as a result of being abused rendered unreliable because the research is done by social sciences? What is the alternative? A scriptural account? Some orthodox theological interpretation?

Does the argument that there are "metaphysical" presuppositions of sociological studies of religion invalidate interpretations of religious institutions and activities by social scientists who study those phenomena? Do not the current social scientific studies of congregations, which assume some naturalistic "metaphysical" presuppositions, provide important information about, and interpretations of, contemporary religion? Is it wrong for church leaders to guide reforms in the light of those findings? Is it not possible that studies made from the criticized functionalist perspectives reveal important aspects of religious life and activity that a scriptural or theological perspective conceals? Remember my opening illustration of the collapsing gallery. Would Jonathan Edwards's providential explanation be a sufficient account of the event? Would the theological and religious meaning he found in it be possible without the naturalistic explanation?

My first solo book, *Treasure in Earthen Vessels: The Church as a Human Community*, was a response to the limitations of scriptural and theological interpretations of the church that were being made in the mid-twentieth century by many famous theologians on the Commission on Christ and the Church of the World Council of Churches.[7] The biblical and theological issues involved in the relations of Christ to the church that elicited books by Anders Nygren, T. F. Torrance, Frederick Dillistone, A. Newton Flew, and others could not explain the institutional political and power structures of the World Council of Churches itself, or the multiple reasons why persons participated in the Northford, Connecticut, Congregational Church I served as pastor and teacher. They did not even illumine, not to mention explain, the major conflicts in the biennial meetings of the General Council of the Congregational Christian Churches in which I participated in the 1950s: the authority and status of its Council for Social Action, and its negotiations with the Evangelical and Reformed Church to form the United Church of Christ. Concepts from political science and sociology explained more institutional difficulties than did the frequent affirmative answer to the oft-repeated question, "Is this merger the will of Christ, or is it not?" Paul Harrison's Weberian sociological analysis *Power and Authority in the Free Church*

Tradition, a study of the American Baptist Convention in the mid-twentieth century, highlights the discrepancy between the uses of power and the theological or institutional authorization for it.[8] The theological treatises did not explain how an identifiable religious community was sustained over time through natural social processes and activities that transmit tradition—processes that also function in the American Legion and the Daughters of the Confederacy. Interestingly, George Lindbeck's cultural-linguistic theological method is adapted from social science sources, principally the work of Clifford Geertz. In my preferred vocabulary that is not a theological method, but a social scientific theory used for a theological purpose.

In pastoral care, what would be the consequences if the postcritical theological critique of the human sciences and other forms of "modernist reasoning" invalidated the use of psychological, social psychological, and other information and concepts in the work of the ministry? It is true that many passages from classic Christian spiritual and pastoral writings show insight and wisdom comparable to modern pastoral care. It is also true that the sciences of the human strengthen intuitive insights, and guide counselors in the thickets of specific problems.

The blanket dismissal of various sciences to explain human nature and activity, and particularly religion and religious activities, is simplistic. Because a complete explanation cannot be validated, the dismissal seems to rule out the importance of partial explanations. It desires to limit the impact of any traffic coming from these sources. My experience is not idiosyncratic; theologically, ethically, and pastorally I have learned much from scholarship about nature, society, history, culture, and especially the human, which is grounded in the project of the Enlightenment. This book, no doubt, in the light of the work of Milbank and the editors of "Radical Traditions," is an example of "a confused array of debates concerning the place of theology in modernity."

The second question I raise about closing religious discourse off from critical revision in light of sciences and other secular discourse is a practical one, noted in the first chapter. I recall it briefly. Not only theologians but moralists, pastors, and laypeople in our culture and time are subjected to alternative accounts, religious and secular, of the same events and actions. They hear a sermon in the morning and watch *Nova* in the evening. They read Mark's story of Jesus calming the storm and watch the Weather Channel's prediction and explanation of a storm in the evening. They have a sense of remorse, if not guilt, for actions that are contrary to God's law, but they read psychological or sociological explanations of it.

In these circumstances religious leadership has choices. It can seek to destroy confidence in the credibility of scientific accounts by criticizing their philosophical presuppositions. What will it substitute for them? Scriptural language? This will hardly help pastors and laypeople, though theologians and academic moralists might be persuaded, especially if they write only for each other. Scholars can avoid the dissonance by arguing for, or assuming, multiple, or at least double, truths that are incommensurable with each other: the truth of faith and the truth of science, for example.

When the discourses from the two realms address the same subject matter, one recommendation is to live in cognitive dissonance, for example, between Edwards's naturalistic and his providential accounts of the collapse of the gallery. Some philosophical theologians might be satisfied: the language of religion and the language of science are incommensurable. But this will not satisfy the college student with whom we walked through courses, or the inquisitive adolescent in a confirmation class, or a reflective professional person who comes to an inquiry class for membership in a congregation. In our pluralistic culture, with its many religious and other ways of interpreting human nature and activity, and many other things, to seek to avoid traffic from the sciences and other secular learning that impinges on religious routes by accepting assumptions of postcritical theology is to retreat into a sectarian religion. This retreat, I believe, has no historical justification in the classic Roman Catholic, Orthodox, Lutheran, Reformed, or Anglican traditions. The first article of the Apostles' Creed, which affirms that God is "the Maker of heaven and earth," necessitates understanding heaven and earth as carefully as possible. Sectarian Christianity, whether in left-wing Protestant, Roman Catholic, Lutheran, Reformed, or Anglican churches, can become either a secure enclave of dogmatic beliefs and esoteric practices, or a source of aggressive attack on "modernist reasoning." Both of these choices evade a clear picture of where many people with religious sensibilities live. Religious leaders should pray a prayer from Kenya:

> From the cowardice that dares not face new truth
> From the laziness that is contented with half truth
> From the arrogance that thinks it knows all truth
> Good Lord, deliver me.[9]

To be so delivered is to accept the burden of the agenda of this book.

2. Accommodation Strategies: "Left-Leaning"

Among examples of accommodation strategies that theologians and others use to deal with scientific and other secular discourse are those that move to the left—that is, toward accepting the scientific accounts as determinative of what can be said theologically. The historically significant work of the Unitarian scholar Ralph Wendell Burhoe and the journal *Zygon* would be sources to examine this tendency and differences among those who share a general trajectory. While most Protestant theology found philosophical and theological devices to avoid taking into account evidence and theories of genetics and other sciences of the human, some members of the *Zygon* group were open to quite radical revisions of religious claims.

To be sure, writers of Christian ethics became somewhat learned about scientific accounts of the human, and accepted them as valid explanations, but usually only to address them more precisely from their versions of ethics. The *theology* of Christian ethics was not revised in the light of secular research; the authority and autonomy of Christian ethics was assumed and sometimes defended. Scientific research gives information about the circumstances in which human intervention was possible, for example, prenatal detection of genetically defective fetuses. On the basis of deductions from *agape* for Paul Ramsey, and from natural law for Roman Catholic moral theologians, precise courses of action could be morally assessed, and immoral ones proscribed. In radical distinction from this, the *Zygon* group believed that scientific learning required revisions in the interpretation of the human, the doctrine of God, and other traditional beliefs. At the extreme, some of that group equated God with the scientifically established laws of nature, and argued that religion could be explained by research into the functions of the right and left hemispheres of the brain. Others leaned toward that extreme, but sought to accommodate traditional Christian teachings to it. A case in point is the work of the Lutheran theologian Philip Hefner.[10]

Hefner's book, *The Human Factor: Evolution, Culture, and Religion*, won the Templeton Foundation Book Award in 1995, an award that, to the best of my knowledge, has always gone to books that find compatibility between traditional religious ideas and theories from contemporary sciences.[11] After showing how Irme Lakatos's philosophical work sets a context for his theological engagement particularly with biological and cultural sciences, Hefner states "the core" of his proposal.

> Human beings are God's created co-creators whose purpose is to be the agency, acting in freedom, to birth the future that is most wholesome for the nature that has birthed us—the nature that is not only our genetic heritage, but also the entire human community and the evolutionary and ecological reality in which and to which we belong. Exercising this agency is said to be God's will for humans.[12]

In every respect this book implies a rejection of the description of the series called "Radical Traditions" and of the fundamental line of Milbank's argument. Its development is complex because it is founded on the descriptive premise of these lectures, namely, that theology and secular sciences address and account for the same phenomena, in this case the human. Hefner's form of my premise is that nature is the matrix of the human, and nature is "God's great project." "For theology, this entails the conclusion that theology is not on track unless it can interpret the traditions of the religious communities as revelation about the natural order."[13] He does not, however, propose my second option of having sciences determine what can be said about God and the human. "God-talk and scientific conceptualizations *may mingle* in our songs of the world in the manner of melody and counterpoint" (italics added). He concludes, *"God-talk should be viewed as expressing something about our experience of a world that is scientifically understood."*[14] The project does not assume that the theological traffic into the human is one-directional like the critique of "modernist reasoning." Rather than theology evading scientific interpretations as Milbank's theological project seeks to do, Hefner's involves incorporating evidences and theories from biological sciences and cultural or social sciences into a theological interpretation. The sciences *in*vade theology, rather than theology *e*vading the sciences. In its development Hefner revises traditional interpretations of Christian doctrines and ethical principles so that they are deeply informed by a biocultural account of the human. In a different way, this could also be called "radical theology."

In this chapter I can only illustrate Hefner's mutual engagement between some of the sciences and theology and ethics. Traffic merges from both a traditional theological direction and a scientific direction into a smoothly flowing pattern. Traditional traffic patterns from theology are redirected to accommodate traffic from the sciences. It is theology done, however one might finally assess its success, in the context of our culture, the world in which educated laity dwell when they are not in church, and the world in which theologians, moralists, pastors at least read about, even if they write and talk theology mostly to one another.

Hefner, like some other theologians, has displaced humans as the sole focus of the theological story. Backing this revision is the emergence of the human within the wider and much longer processes of nature as these are explained by evolutionary and anthropological sciences. His chapter "Nature as the Matrix of the Human" draws on some of his hypotheses: "Integral to *Homo sapiens* and its evolutionary history are certain structures and processes, the requirements for whose functioning may be said to constitute, at least in a tentative way, goals and purposes for human life." The meaning and purpose of human beings are "conceived in terms of their placement *within* natural processes and their contributions to those same processes" (italics added).[15] He states a traditional objection to his position, namely, that human meaning and purpose "derive from otherworldly sources of revelation rather than from within nature itself." His response illustrates how he takes scientific accounts of nature and the human to be necessary for a cogent contemporary theology: "whatever assumes the status of religious revelation must now be conceived as knowledge that emerges from nature and whose content is about nature."[16] Our source for knowledge about nature is not, of course, Aristotle, whose interpretation was suffused into the medieval theology of St. Thomas, but contemporary sciences. Hefner can write about humans as co-creators with God, but the context of human creation is the realm of nature. "[W]hatever humans do in their culture-creating and culture-enacting must be referred to the natural order that is their source and ambiance. . . . God's will for us humans transpires within the larger realm of the divine will for the entire natural order, as creation. . . . [W]hatever it means for humans to find fulfillment, which . . . includes love, justice, peace, and the like . . . must be defined within the larger framework of the natural order."[17]

Nature, known through contemporary sciences, is the medium, the realm, the reality through which God works. Hefner, please note, does not argue the most radical position, which claims that what might be said about God must be inferred logically from natural laws and scientific research. His position, though relying heavily on scientific accounts, is still one of accommodation. Information and theories from the sciences *authorize but do not completely determine* his theological and religious interpretations. Religious faith and concepts of God must be poured into the earthen vessel of nature. "The most important thing we can say about our faith and belief in God is that they require us to believe that nature is indeed a realm of grace."[18] But Hefner's level of generality in this book is such that he does not confront the denser, detailed examples used to illustrate the beginning of this book. In what way would the natural processes of the collapsing gallery in Northampton be for Hefner a realm of grace? In the same way they were for Edwards? That is, the fact that no one was killed in the process showed evidence of God's providence? What inferences can one draw from Hefner's interpretation of nature as that through which grace is at work for Calvin's observation that some mothers lactate sufficiently and others do not?

To further illustrate Hefner's project, I sketch briefly one example of a specific historic Christian doctrine, sin, and one example of its outcome for Christian ethics, the love command. Hefner's chapter entitled "Biological Perspectives on Original Sin" begins with a brief account of traditional interpretations of the fall and original sin. From this he turns to a scientifically informed discussion of the dissonance between genes and culture which closes with a comparison between his position and Augustine's. "Contrary to [Augustine's] explanations . . . guilt does not flow as a consequence of an initial sin, but rather is grounded in the evolutionary history and nature of *Homo sapiens*."[19]

This generalization is backed by an adaptation of the work of an evolutionary theorist, Donald T. Campbell, whose contributions to *Zygon* demonstrate interests he shares with religious thinkers. Campbell interprets contemporary urban civilization to be the outcome of the concomitant biological and sociocultural evaluations, an outcome that has behavioral and experiential consequences. There is an inevitable tension in sociocultural evolution between biologically driven dispositions and the requirements of human social systems. This process makes evolutionary sense out of religious interpretations of temptation and original sin. Hefner quotes Campbell, "The commandments, the proverbs, the religious 'law' represent social-evolutionary products directed at inculcating tendencies that are in direct opposition to the 'temptations' which for the most part represent dispositional tendencies produced by biological evolution. For every commandment we may reasonably hypothesize a biological tendency running counter to some social-systematic optimum."[20]

The "mythic symbol of the fall" correlates with the tensions that are inevitably present in the interaction of "two information systems," the genetic and the cultural, that are basic both to the human individual and to social existence. Against the criticism that this reduces "sin" to bland fallibility and finitude, Hefner avers that these tensions are the "underlying ground of sin" in its most virulent expressions. Hefner's interpretation of human freedom coheres with his interpretation of sin. "Freedom is . . . defined as the capacity to launch into, and to persist in, the trial-and-error program that evolution sets for us" and that is "intrinsic to the human central nervous system."[21] (The full discussion of freedom is found in a previous chapter, "Freedom and Determinism in Evolutionary Perspective.") The sciences and the mythic religious symbolism of sin mutually enrich each other; the religious symbols are commensurate with the scientific accounts, and the scientific accounts "deepen" the religious interpretation.

Hefner wants it understood that his position does not claim that theories from the sciences determine theology. He explicitly rejects this: "I make these comments not simply on the assumption that science determines what may or may not be believed religiously."[22] The alternative to scientific determination, however, is not the extrinsic or objective authority of biblical or traditional theology. Rather, taking his cues from Paul Ricoeur, it is that the symbols of the religious tradition are "primordial readings of human experience and the human position within the natural and social world." The test of the tradition is its revelatory power with reference to human experience. Whether the religious tradition "is enhanced or rendered obsolete when juxtaposed to science is . . . dependent upon whether the symbol seems to render adequately what accounts as *significant* human experience, inclusive of science" (italics added).[23]

Hefner's ideas were introduced above by stating that his project is a kind of accommodation between information and theories from contemporary sciences and traditional theology. He explicitly denies that his position is one in which theological and religious discourse is determined by the sciences. But his accommodating position is not an easy compatibility between traditional religious ideas and the scientific. Does it require a radical rejection of some important Christian beliefs? If Augustine's interpretation of sin is one of those beliefs, the answer is affirmative. Rather than engaging in an aggressive polemic against traditional theology from the scientific sources, Hefner reroutes the theological smoothly—retaining as much of its traditional course as possible while altering the traffic that it bears. Hefner's enterprise in theology moves a full 180 degrees from Milbank's. It is, no doubt, one party in the "confused array of debates concerning the place of theology in modernity" that the series "Radical Traditions: Theology in a Postcritical Key" promises to resolve.

In addition to doctrine, Hefner explores the significance of his left-leaning accommodation for Christian ethics. I noted above that many authors of Christian ethics seek to understand how the sciences describe and explain circumstances in which moral choices are made. How does *agape* apply to prenatal diagnosis of a genetically transmitted disease? One has to know enough genetics to make a cogent moral argument for or against a particular intervention. Similarly, how does natural law apply? The traffic is one-directional, from Christian ethics to the sciences. Neither Christian ethics nor its supporting theology is revised. For Hefner, they are.

A clue to how Hefner finds naturalistic support for the love command is found in his brief interpretation of the Beatitudes. They are an expression of the character of nature. They present "a picture of what the wisest, most adequate human life would look like, the life that is most fully in accord with the fundamental nature of reality."[24] What is conveyed in the Beatitudes "is that *reality does possess a fundamental nature, and that human life ought to be in accord with that fundamental nature.*"[25] The blessings are not some special gift of grace given by God, but the fulfillment of life in accord with nature. "Meekness is in accord with the fundamental nature of reality, and it will find resonance with the coherence that accords with nature."[26] The love command is not contrary to nature, but fundamentally in accord with nature.

In Hefner's work, one is not surprised that his first two chapters on the love command synthesize an evolutionary background for values and morality. The roots of values and morality "indeed go deep, even into the prehistory of nerve and sinew."[27] They emerged as a necessity for life and its evolution. Various theorists of evolution are cited and evaluated, all of them generally supporting his interpretation that humans as co-creators developed in the course of evolution. As the "new conditions" of humanity emerged, culture developed; humans had to fashion a system of information and guidance that is comparable to and integrated into "the physico-biogenetic systems that preceded it in the evolutionary process and that continued to coexist with *Homo sapiens.*"[28]

Before turning to a scientific assessment of the love command, Hefner briefly develops the essential characteristics of the "Christian myth": creation by God, human alienation, the conveying of grace and its moral consequences in Jesus, and resurrection that assures the perfection and consummation of the entire created order.[29] The most appropriate response "to this casting of the symbolic universe" and its imperative to action is the Great Commandment, "You shall love the Lord your God with all your heart, and with all your soul, and with all your mind . . . and . . . you shall love your neighbor as yourself" (Matt. 22:37ff.). This biblical language "translates into" a naturalistic interpretation of the place of the human in the ordering of nature, suffused with a fabric of mystery that is finally grounded in a coherent reality that, as I understand Hefner, is

God. To love God is to have awe and regard for "the central reality" and adapt ourselves to it by taking regard for all its ways. To love this reality is to live "in commitment and accountability to it." Love of neighbor "translates into" solidarity with the entire human community unlimited by any social demarcations, and into unreserved action on behalf of other humans.

His "translated" summary of the love commandment, then, is as follows: "the reality system of nature in which we live is itself basically an ambiance in which we truly belong, an ambiance that has brought us into being and that enables us to fill the purposes for which we were brought into being. The central reality that undergirds all of concrete experience and to which we continually seek to adapt is disposed toward us in a way that we can interpret as graciousness and beneficent support. . . . [O]ur moral action . . . is our way of living in harmony with the way things really are." The love command as "the all-encompassing symbolic universe" functions as myth, that is, it discloses how things really are.[30] Thus scientific studies and religious myths "converge." Religious believers should not be disturbed by this; it is not a perversion of religious truth or a functionalist reductionism. "Rather, on the one hand the scientific statements are prophetic, reminding the religious communities of the deeper significance of their heritage. On the other hand, the mythic stance in general and the Christian myth in particular would predict that the scientists would come to their conclusions. In general, the mythic view believes that it speaks of the way things really are, and if the love command is central to the myth, it will appear central to scientific study of finite phenomena."[31]

My selections from Hefner's book and my summaries encompass neither the variety of sources he uses nor his synthesis of them into a generally coherent position. As I noted, his position is an accommodation strategy that "leans to the left." The sciences do not so much *limit* his theological interpretation of the human as they *authorize* without completely determining it. That is, it relies heavily on the validity and reliability of general lines of evolutionary interpretations of the universe, of biological life, and especially the human. It is also informed by studies of myth by anthropologists, and especially by the philosopher Paul Ricoeur. That is, Hefner synthesizes a *naturalistic description and explanation* of the emergence of the human, and of human activity. Specifically, how does this synthesis of theories from the sciences intersect with his theological account of the human? He seems not simply to reinterpret the science with a religious meaning drawn from Christian tradition.

Hefner uses metaphors at times: the theological and the scientific "mingle in our songs of the world in the manner of melody and counterpoint." "Harmony" is used from time to time. But he articulates his view in less metaphorical terms as well. "God-talk" should express "something about our experience of a world that is scientifically understood." For ethics, God's moral will "transpires *within the larger realm* of the divine will *for the entire natural order.*" The natural order, scientifically explained, is that through which God's moral will for humans is to be interpreted. More specifically, Christian ethics of love refers to the proper ordering of the human in relation to the natural order. On the basis of the sciences, Hefner proposes a test of a religious tradition: whether its symbols seem "to render adequately what accounts as significant human experience, inclusive of science." Yet he also seems to deny that "science determines what may or may not be believed religiously." He does not, in my judgment, claim an orthodox authorization for Christianity based on a special divine revelation given finally and exclusively in Christian Scriptures and in Christ. But he would not be satisfied with a gap the reader has to fill between a scientific narrative and religious reflections on it, which his friend Ursula Goodnenough (an active member of a Presbyterian church and a professor of biology) leaves in her meditative book *The Sacred Depths of Nature*.[32] A clue to how he uses religious tradition is his inclusion of the Christian story in a larger category of mythic accounts.

Hefner's account of the intersection of the sciences and theology and ethics issues in midrange generalizations. Hefner uses no illustrations as specific as the collapse of the gallery in Northampton, or Calvin's account of lactation. He does not test his account, in this book, in specific and dense scientific accounts: genetic determination of particular diseases, or scientific explanations of the pollution of the natural environment. Natural and moral evils do not get prominent attention; thus whether pain and suffering, or catastrophic natural events can cohere with the assurance that the natural order graciously and beneficently supports life is not confronted. Also, he does not engage in deciding what action in accord with reality might be correct in specific circumstances. What action in accord with reality is required when there is a prenatal diagnosis of a genetic disorder such as Tay-Sachs disease, when abortion of the fetus is the only way to avoid a debilitating and fatal disease of childhood? What action is in accord with the evidence that PCBs emitted in industrial economies causes global warming?

But Hefner's is not a metaphysical account on the level of abstraction and universality of many process theologians. He does not give an exposition of the primordial and consequent natures of God, or an abstract description of reality as a social process. The synthesis is in a middle range between the abstract metaphysical and the very specifically empirical. What we do have, as I noted, is 180 degrees away from the rejections of the human sciences for purposes of theology in Milbank and the description of the book series "Radical Traditions."

In this example of an accommodation strategy between sciences and religious discourse, what finally trumps what? Hefner does not engage in the radical philosophical critique of the human sciences that Milbank does, though from the text it is clear that he knows the literature that informs Milbank. Carefully critical comments assure the reader that Hefner is not a scientific fundamentalist. He acknowledges the limits of science. He does not explicitly confront the issue of whether God, as the mysterious orderer of nature, can still be spoken of as a person who makes choices and can will to interrupt natural processes in response to intercessions. Nor does Hefner engage in a radical scientific debunking of religious beliefs such as Steven Weinberg, Richard Dawkins, and others delight in making. Hefner's work can be differentiated from that of Daniel Day Williams, who used process thinking to expound the central messages of the Christian Scriptures. Hefner's use of the sciences is not a homiletical device to show contemporary scientifically informed persons what Christian theology means in our time.

Does Hefner's use of the sciences, to be sure on a general level, *reinterpret* Christian theology? It seems to me that a *scientific* interpretation of nature and human experience is accepted, and that the *mythic* interpretation of religious symbol systems justifies his compatibilism between Christian religious discourse and the sciences. An accommodation from the left does not lead to denial of the truth of religious symbols, but finds compatibility with them. The sciences do not limit what Hefner says about God and God's relations to the world. Rather, they authorize but do not fully determine his use of religious language.

Later in this chapter, other examples of accommodation, not "left-leaning" like Hefner's, are analyzed.

Two sharply contrasting interpretations of the intersection of naturalistic or scientific and theological accounts have been analyzed. The ideal-type of rejection illumines the description of a series of books edited by Stanley Hauerwas and Peter Ochs, "Radical Traditions: Theology in a Postcritical Key," and John Milbank's *Theology and Social Theory*. Philip Hefner's *The Human Factor: Evolution, Culture, and Religion* is illumined by the absorption type, particularly in the form in which the sciences authorize but do not limit a theological interpretation.

Hefner would have to reject Milbank's philosophical and theological position. Milbank and Hauerwas and Ochs would accuse Hefner of surrendering to "the Enlightenment project," and thus contributing to the "confused array of debates concerning the place of theology in modernity." The rejection clears the way for scriptural hegemony, for radical orthodoxy or unapologetic theology, even if such makes religious discourse unintelligible to scholars of secular disciplines and to many persons in contemporary westernized societies and cultures, and at least problematic to many members of Christian churches. Whatever one's assessment of Hefner's account, it is clear that he believes both the sciences and theology address the same phenomenon: the human. From this he infers that some far-reaching revision of theology and other religious discourse is necessary. The secular scientific accounts are given much more immediate and direct theological significance than in Edward Farley's and Karl Barth's accommodation positions analyzed in this chapter. It is instructive to see how these theologians accommodate secular accounts in very different ways. Both, however, accept their positive contributions.

3. Accommodation Strategies: A Centrist Position

One strategy used by theologians formulates a *philosophical* account of the human that draws both from the sciences and from the experience of human agency and freedom. A *description* of the persisting and distinguishing characteristics of the human is developed by inferences from several realms of human experience and knowledge: the sciences of the human, the experience of freedom and the capacity to take initiatives, and our interhuman subjective experiences. This account stands on its own, so to speak, and can be evaluated for its adequacy as such. It depends for its justification neither on the degree of scientific authorization Hefner uses nor on a scriptural or theological authorization that one is left with by the rejection extreme. In effect, the evidences and arguments are mixed. Once the description and explanation are established, they can be penetrated by a theological interpretation. Books by two American contemporaries take this general trajectory, although in quite different ways: Gordon Kaufman's *In the Face of Mystery: A Constructive Theology* and Edward Farley's *Good and Evil: Interpreting a Human Condition.*[33] An analysis of the most relevant parts of Farley's book, and remarks on it, will suffice for this chapter.

Farley frames part of his project in terms similar to those used in this book. After he makes clear that his ontology of the human takes several "spheres" into account, the interhuman, the social institutional, and the personal, he addresses the "biological aspect of the personal." He is fully cognizant of the critical philosophy that backs Milbank's interpretation and argues against its sufficiency. He is equally critical of biological reductionism. Its focused research tends to deny the full complexity of the human; "human being is the physiological operations of the brain"; it suppresses human capacities for "self-initiation"; and metaphysically it presupposes a concept of reality as such, as physical and mundane.[34] The human as "personal being" is the focus of his interpretation. The biological is one aspect of the human.

This is in contrast to Hefner, who focuses on the biological and interprets the personal in the light of biological sciences. Both Farley and Hefner, however, formulate accounts that are intentionally multidimensional; both seek to avoid what Farley calls "the ghost of Mani" that haunts Christian theology by interpreting the distinctiveness of the human "as something floating above nature and the body."[35] Christian theology began "to formulate its revelational or Scriptural version of human good and evil as if they had no relation whatever to the awesome realities studied by neurophysiology, microbiology, and sociobiology."[36] Both Farley and Hefner concur in the descriptive premise of this book: the same phenomena addressed by theological and ethical discourse are addressed by other academic disciplines.

The failure of theology to relate to the awesome biological sciences might protect the region of faith, but it leads to some unfortunate choices. Farley frames the issues in terms congenial to this book. One option is that the human being described by the sciences is "the real human being," and, for example, what the religious tradition has called sin can be scientifically explained. This is the type I call absorption. Another option is that the sciences have no bearing on a theological interpretation. The human is something spiritual or mental that flies over the causalities explained by the sciences. This is the type I call rejection. Farley's third option from the tradition is dualism: both the scientific and the theological accounts are real, but have nothing to do with each other.[37] This is the cognitive dissonance that I discussed as one form of rejection. Farley seeks to avoid all three options.

To overcome the insufficiencies of each, Farley uses the metaphor of dimensions. The biological is a *dimension* of human agency. (He also uses "aspect." Whether the words are used synonymously is unclear.) Note: human agency, the personal, the capacity for initiation, and the realm of the interpersonal and social are the most characteristic of the human. The biological is one dimension of the person. Hefner, in contrast, comes close to interpreting the personal, the capacity for agency, and the interpersonal and social as outcomes, or even "dimensions," of the biological. Both Hefner's and Farley's are accommodation positions; both want an account of the human that is informed by contemporary sciences. In Farley's account, however, the biological is not as determinative of his philosophical interpretation, which subsequently is interpreted theologically. Hefner's use of the scientific evidences and theories formatively shapes *The Human Factor* and a theological interpretation of it, but they do not exhaust it.

One difficulty theologians and other humanists have in taking account of the sciences is conceptual and verbal. What terms most appropriately express the relationship of the brain to the mind, of biological conditions to intentional human action? If the biological is a dimension of the human, how does one precisely describe and explain the relationship between biology and human responsiveness and agency? Farley's text and notes show that he has read influential writings by scientists and philosophers who focus on this relationship, for examples, Melvin Konner's *The Tangled Wing: Biological Constraints on the Human Spirit* and Mary Midgley's *Beast and Man: The Roots of Human Nature*.[38] He prudently does not attempt to adjudicate controverted issues within the sciences. Farley knows that there are disputes among neuroscientists about the relationship between brain and mind, but he does not argue for or against eliminative materialism, nor for or against the dual interactionism of Sir John Eccles on scientific grounds. He recurs to his types of interpretation in several places. He rejects "biologism."

But, more significantly, he also rejects a "weak view" of the importance of biology, one in which "genetic factors are limited to anatomical features, including the complex structures of the brain, but do not apply to distinctive features of human nature." The weak view interprets the biological only as a necessary condition for human powers; it is only the "background" and "bearer" of our human nature, "the ashes from which the phoenix of our distinctive being arises."[39] This weak view, he asserts, "simply cannot survive in the face of recent decades of genetics, neuropsychology, and sociobiology." Farley wants a deeper penetration of the biological dimension in the human than the weak view permits.[40] His position is a modification of one type described in the first chapter; the scientific account authorizes a description and explanation of the human, but its use in a philosophical anthropology is sharply limited. The biological is a dimension of the personal; the personal is not a dimension of the biological. The sciences require an alteration in the philosophical, theological, and ethical claims that reflect "the ghost of Mani," but they are not as determinative of those claims as Hefner argues.

In his desire to accommodate a philosophy of the human to the sciences, Farley, like others, uses ambiguous terms, perhaps intentionally. "The *condition* of human agents, whatever else it is, is the condition of living animals" (italics added). Animality, our being mammals and primates, is not left behind "by *whatever* constitutes human agency" (italics added). "Ciphers of transcendence," such as love and evil, are "not *simply* terms for physiological states," but "occur *in conjunction with* a living organism" (italics added). The organic is *not just a theoretical hypothesis* of the human condition; it is an aspect of it" (italics added). "[T]he biological is a certain *facticity* of human reality along with the facticities of the interhuman and the societal" (italics added). The biological dimension "does not occur prior or even alongside of these other facticities but *pervades* and *influences* them" (italics added).[41] Farley's various verbalizations of the relationship between the scientifically described and explained aspects of the human and the distinctive capacities for agency are noted to show how difficult it is for anyone precisely to conceptualize and articulate a position that avoids biologism, the ghost of Mani, and dualism.

Farley's argument is developed in greater detail, and in various dimensions, all of which cohere in his accommodation position. His account of maturation, reproduction, the biological unconscious, flexibility, and kinship is, in effect, a composite of the sciences that pertain most to his interpretation of the human. The philosopher/theologian engages in a summary account that can be judged for its accuracy and adequacy by biologists. From these he comes to a conclusion, again one that can be assessed by scientists. The evidences and theories converge in a biological statement about the human: "a single dynamic, the biological condition of human agents is marked by striving in an environment that is both supportive and threatening."[42] This is not a theological conclusion; it is a summary of biological evidences and theories. It is integrated, however, into the further philosophical/theological interpretation of the human condition.

In a further statement one sees how Farley moves toward his phenomenological and theological interpretation. "[I]n its biological sense, the human agent is a living animal who strives to maintain the conditions of its existence and to obtain its organically rooted satisfactions in an indifferent and dangerous world. Accordingly, it is biochemically and morphologically equipped to oppose, fight back, and attack. Our biology, in other words, disposes us toward a range of satisfactions and equips us to oppose whatever threatens to remove them."[43] The interpretations of the tragic, of good and evil, and of redemption that follow in the book integrate the biological into the personal and interpersonal dimensions.

It is important to reiterate: this is not a theological account. No theological interpretation is apparent in part 1 of Farley's book. There is no appeal to Christian Scriptures or to the theological tradition to warrant what he argues. Only after he has described the "elemental passions," the deep desires that presumably all humans have for "subjectivity," for the "interhuman," and for "reality" and their consequent tragic structure does Farley introduce theology. Only then can the question be raised about whether God is the referent of those passions. He makes his moves with care. There is a fourth passion, "a single eros for the eternal," but this does not warrant the simple deduction that God is its referent. "The eternal horizon of the passions is not simply a nothingness but is whatever would fulfill the passions." This is *not* a generalization that could be assessed biologically. Apart from "the human passion for the eternal," however, there could be no question of God. "It is only because we are able to passionately desire through our penultimate satisfactions that the very notion of God is meaningful."[44] Clearly he has extrapolated from his biological account to a theological horizon.

In the second part of his book Farley develops traditional Christian theological themes of good and evil, idolatry, redemption, and others in ways consonant with the ontology of the human fashioned in the first part. The critical question a reader asks is whether his interpretations are scientifically informed philosophical terms for biblical and traditional theological beliefs and concepts, or whether their relationship to traditional Christian language is incidental. A clear difference from Hefner's work exists: Farley does not correlate his scientifically informed interpretation with explicitly biblical or theological language as Hefner does.

A comparison of their discussions of *agape* is to the point. I have described Hefner's interpretation of Christian love and the love commandment. His approach, basically, is to take the relevant New Testament texts on the one hand, and on the other his biologically informed understanding of the human to show that the biblical is supported by the scientific. This requires a scientific interpretation of the biblical language. Farley's interpretation of *agape* is much too complex to expound here. Suffice it to say that it is impregnated with phenomenology, and particularly with concepts and vocabulary adapted from the writings of Emmanuel Levinas. He eschews any traditional theology of *agape* that claims it to be the effect of supernatural grace. Rather, he makes a case for *agape* as being present in ordinary human experience as "communion." "Agapic relation is a relation of both compassionate obligation and mutually appreciating affection." In his more technical language, it is "a relation of face in the fullest sense of face and is present wherever human beings are thous to each other in that sense."[45]

Both Hefner and Farley naturalize *agape*. In Hefner's case biology more directly shapes his account. He has more at stake in arguing that *agape* is grounded in fundamental human biological life. In Farley's case biology is a dimension of the personal, and his philosophy of the human, informed by Continental phenomenology, determines what he says. His view of *agape* as communion rests more on a phenomenology adapted from Levinas than on biology.

Although the title of Farley's book is *Good and Evil*, inferences from his argument that would address particular controverted practical moral questions do not come into its purview. His invocation of biological sciences is at a general level; while he knows that there are implications from neuroscience, for example, for traditional issues of freedom and the capacity for self-initiation, he does not examine them microscopically. Nor does he even hint at a "physico-theology" that would look for the relations of divine causality to biological explanations, something Hefner does. But his argument accommodates scientific evidences and explanations into an account of the human, without their determining it. While the project is philosophical, his argument is against theologically supported dualisms. The neurosciences, molecular genetics, and other sciences have implications for modern theology. I infer that Farley would be quite dissatisfied with discussions of the relations of theology and ethics to secular knowledge that focus only on abstract epistemological and methodological issues. Whatever one's final assessment of Farley's project, it is clear that contemporary philosophical theology must be substantially informed by, among other things, the sciences of the human.

A Brief Excursus

Before turning to the final section on the human sciences and theology, which is a selection from Karl Barth's *Church Dogmatics*, readers should remember that other sciences intersect with theology and ethics. In a parallel way, critical analysis of them in possible.

One procedure is various strands of theology and ethics accepts scientific accounts of phenomena, whether natural or historical, and then *reinterprets* them to give a religious or moral meaning. No quarrel is required with the sciences. Edwards's narrative of the collapse of the gallery is an example. A naturalistic explanation of its causes is given; a theological account gives religious meaning to the natural event. What was explained "scientifically" was also an act of the special providence of God.

A similar procedure has been practiced in liberation and other theologies and ethics. Accounts of social, economic, and political conditions that oppress women, racial minorities, and the poor are one phase. Social scientific and historical studies are often adduced to support them. Descriptions and explanations are adapted from economics, political science, and secular philosophy. In liberation theologies Marxist accounts were often judged to provide the most adequate comprehensive interpretation. Neither libertarian free market theories nor accounts of the common good that legitimated a social hierarchy were used. This phase also discloses the *meaning* of oppression for persons and communities: its denigration of human dignity, its outcomes of poor health and education, and unrest that it causes. The consequences are "dehumanizing"—both a description and an evaluation deduced from the evidences.

But a deeper theological and ethical interpretation is given. The evil of "dehumanization" is contrary to what God wills human life to be. Exodus narratives and religious beliefs about sin, redemption, and eschatology support that conviction. Historical analogies are drawn between the bondage of the Hebrew people in Egypt and conditions of oppressed people in our time. A religious and moral imperative is drawn. Just as Yahweh willed their liberation, so God wills the liberation of the currently oppressed. Christians should be engaged in the liberation of all oppressed groups. Evil is "structural"; the sins of the powerful create the human misery of the oppressed. Or, the newness of all things in Christ requires historical actualization and radical social change. The obligation of Christian churches and groups is to be agents of God's liberating purposes and activity, or, in Paul Lehmann's terms, of "what God is doing to make and keep human life human." In some instances social sciences inform economic, political, and military policies that actualize God's liberating or humanizing purposes. The intersection of institutional power and action with God's power and action in conditions of oppression and liberation could be analyzed similarly to the analyses of the human in this chapter. What do theologians and Christian social reformers reject, absorb, or accommodate from the social science studies? And how do they justify their choices?

Such a scenario can be examined at several levels. Many different questions can be asked to refine the query. Are the descriptions and explanations of oppression, whether political, economic, sexist, or racial, comprehensive and accurate? Have important factors been omitted? What determines the order of importance of included factors? What gives coherence to the scenario? Has a moral or religious bias distorted the interpretation?

What secular social and political theories are appropriate? Is a Marxist one the best? Or, is Talcott Parsons's theory of social structures and processes more accurate? On this matter, at issue is a debate between social scientific interpretations. A theologian has to judge a debate among social theorists. Is one a more accurate account of God's purposes than the other?

What ethical and theological concepts are chosen to interpret events and circumstances explained by social and behavioral sciences? Which theory of justice is chosen, John Rawls's, or that of communitarian views which give the common good priority? Is the concept of sin, as used by Reinhold Niebuhr, to be

preferred to an eschatological theology and ethics of hope, as in Jürgen Moltmann's writings? Would a retrieval of natural law, as in the work of Jacques Ma-
ritain, suffice? Does a theologian choose the concepts and theories that are
most congenial to his or her religious and moral interests?

Theology and the sciences intersect in ethical and theological concerns for
social well-being, and in every specific circumstance and proposed reform. It is
fair, from a scholarly perspective, to insist that these questions be answered as
self-consciously as possible. A justification will use mixed warrants, necessarily,
unless the choice of a comprehensive theory, for example, Marxism, determines
the relevance of the social science accounts. The agenda of this book is applicable to other theological and ethics concerns than the human.

4. Accommodation Strategies: Reject, Reorient, Reinterpret

Hefner's and Farley's arguments accurately represent stages of Karl Barth's long
discussion of "Phenomenal Man" and "Real Man." A scientifically based naturalism, an ethical perspective, and an anthropology that opens toward theism.
They are only parts of what Barth calls "phenomenal man." He does not deny
that each of these says something about the human, but they are judged to be
totally inadequate to understand "real man." Here I examine parts of Barth's
sections "The Phenomenon of the Human" and "Real Man" in *Church Dogmatics*,
III/2, *The Doctrine of Creation*.[46] The entire volume is pertinent to this book; the
parts on which I focus illustrate a radically critical, but finally not dismissive,
use of secular accounts of the human. In a fashion that Barth uses in other
areas, he radically undercuts reliance on human knowledge and actions in
order to make his strongest claims for a theology of revelation. Once that is secure, from its perspective what was criticized can be reinterpreted in its light.
The nub of his argument can be simply stated: any interpretation of the human
in relation to nature, to morality, and other similar contexts cannot grasp the
"real man." At best, when used by religious thinkers as starting points, they are
only openings toward God. The real human can be understood only on the basis
of a christological account of God's initiative, and in relation to God.

Critical questions, to which I shall return, are first, whether Barth's interpretation of "real man" is based on a particularistic revelational authority that
is exempt from criticism or correction by secular scholarship; second, can theologians, pastors, or laypersons render this theology intelligible (not to mention persuasive) to persons who use secular discourse to understand the
human? Would the college student in the second chapter be persuaded by her
religion instructor or pastor that only in relation to Jesus can she know the real
nature of the human? Could Barth's interpretation of real man even be made intelligible to neuroscientists, geneticists, economists, novelists, and others?

There is no equivocation in Barth's claim that rightly to understand the
nature of the human one must accept his christological starting point. "[W]e

cannot compromise with those who think they can know the nature of man on other grounds than those which are legitimate for us. These minimal requirements are given us by our christological basis." "[T]here can be no question of an understanding of man from which the idea of God is excluded."[47] This is stated forthrightly before he examines alternative views, all of which only explain aspects of "phenomenal man." Then, after developing an extensive theological anthropology, he returns briefly to reinterpret these alternatives in light of his theology. But the knowledge of the real human is attainable *only* from the standpoint of knowledge of God.

Barth summarizes six criteria for evaluating other interpretations, all based on his Christology. All have the same logical structure: if (a) is true, then (b) necessarily follows. If the Christology is true, then certain things follow that are true about all humans. One of the six is: "If it is the case in relation to the man Jesus that the presence and revelation of God in Him is the history of deliverance of each and every man, then necessarily, assuming that there is similarity between Him and us, every man is a being in history which stands in a clear and recognizable relationship to the divine deliverance enacted in the man Jesus."[48] This and the other five "are the limits within which we shall always have to move in our search" for "real man."[49]

With these criteria in mind, Barth examines other scholarly efforts to comprehend the nature of the human: biological naturalism, ethics, existentialism, and theism. Each of these accounts for something significant, and each points beyond its limitations toward a more adequate view. But all are based on understanding the human autonomously, not in relation to what God has revealed about the human. Samples of Barth's extensive, verbose, and repetitive arguments suffice to show a theological accommodation to secular descriptions and explanations, while *only* theology knows the real or true nature of the human.

The first viewpoint that Barth discusses, only to reject, is any theology that uses a naturalistic interpretation of the human based on sciences. Recall Philip Hefner's theology. From Barth's christological criteria, human self-knowledge based on "immediately accessible and knowable characteristics of the nature" that all persons share "must be regarded as a vicious circle" that never gets to the real human. Before he completes his demolition of scientific naturalism, however, he slightly qualifies his negative judgment. "We cannot and will not dispute that he sees and grasps something which *perhaps indicates* the nature of true man" (italics added). What is grasped by the sciences may show "symptoms" of the real human.[50]

Barth does not build his case by citing theological writings that adduced naturalistic explanations in their arguments, or on the sciences directly. Again, recall Hefner's work as a contemporary case in point. Barth cites, for example, a theological text that accepts the theory that humans are descended from "an extinct simian race of pre-historic times, closely related to the small-nosed apes of Africa and East India."[51] Theologians who do that are judged to be apologists who "undoubtedly applied themselves seriously and fundamentally to the question of human phenomena." But their perspective is limited because they work "within the framework of the biologico-psychological problem," which from Barth's perspective comes from "opponents" to correct theology. This said, he again admits that many of the scientific ideas they use are "both incontestable and important."[52] Humans, he reassures the reader, "must certainly be viewed" in this manner. But the theologians he criticizes "went too far in their basic recognition of the idea of evolution." True, humans must see themselves in relation to animals, but "it is clearly advisable not to remain in this position." "Otherwise" humankind "will not be viewed as a whole."[53]

To support his view of limitations, however, Barth appeals not only to his christocentric theology, but also to the uncertainties of the sciences. Theologians who developed their view on the basis of the biology share "the arrogance of the Darwinians as a secure basis for all further progress. And . . . they thought it their duty to complete and transcend those theories" by adding to them "the further dogma of man as an intellectual and cultural being."[54] So what, in the end, is the significance of what is known from a naturalistic perspective? It is conditioned and relative knowledge that tempts persons to think they can know the nature of the human by seeing what it has in common with animals and the rest of creation.[55] Barth appeals to experience to support his critique; we experience ourselves on other levels, such as freedom—persons who make decisions and act. Thus an examination of the real human looks beyond our biological nature.

This opens to the perspective of ethical considerations and moral experience. Recall Hefner's explanation of the ethical as developing out of the biological, and Farley's account of the personal that draws heavily on moral experience. Barth avers that knowledge of the ethical cannot be deprecated; indeed it "may well be supremely symptomatic" of "real man." His argument is developed in a long excursus on Fichte, and thus he names the second stage "idealism." Humans cannot examine themselves without completing a naturalistic account in addition to an ethical account. This is good, "[b]ut it is not so good that we may think we have attained to real man, to his uniqueness in creation."[56] It fails to tell us whether God even exists, not to mention how God has initiated a relation to humans. "The ethical understanding of man is at one with the naturalistic in visualising man as a self-contained reality."[57] Naturalism views the human from the standpoint of external conditioning; the ethical views the human from the standpoint of inner freedom. Both of these must be "transcended," and both open toward existentialism.

Barth's description of how an existentialist view opens to a theistic anthropology has affinities with Farley's interpretation. Barth reminds the reader of what he had already analyzed. "[A]n organic-chemico-physico" account "is easily demonstrated on the level of the natural sciences." Ethical terms account for "a sequence of actions wrought through time." "And the whole point of the

existential analysis is to understand the distinctive being in man . . . as a striving after being which is to be described as questioning, self-transcendence or
anxiety."[58] This "actualist anthropology" deepens an account of the phenomenal human. It is a fuller account of freedom, responsibility, historicity—in short
of the human capacity to make decisions. It shows that humans can constantly
seize their own possibilities. But it "does not necessarily demand divine instruction," and is still an autonomous rather than a theonomous intepretation.

As in Farley's ontology of the human, in the actualist view "something like
God may be understood," but not necessarily God. The "other" might be "a
vague summary of everything that from man's point of view confronts him and
is superior to him." It might be "the impersonal reality of death as the limit of
human life." It might be another person. But the idea of some "other" distinct
from the human, "even if this other is taken to be God or something like [God],"
is not bound to a specific idea of God, for example, the Christian idea.[59] All we
have is the possibility of the human, an abstract account of capacity, or disposi-
tion, or potentiality. While "the concept of the actuality of man" deepens Barth's
account, "it has not led us any nearer our goal."

Throughout Barth's analysis he reminds the reader of the basis for understanding "real man." His major section, "Real Man," restates and elaborates on
the significance of his christological position. The starting point for understanding the real human is the man Jesus. Any anthropology that poses and answers the question of the true being of the human on any other basis misses the
mark. "Basically and comprehensively . . . to be a man is to be with God. What a
man is in this Counterpart is obviously the basis and comprehensive determination of his true being. Whatever else he is, he is on the basis of the fact that he
is with Jesus and therefore with God."[60] It is "the gracious divine election of the
man Jesus" that determines the truly human. "What is man?" again Barth asks.
"And we answer: he is the being whose Kinsman, Neighbour and Brother is the
man Jesus, and in whose sphere therefore his history takes place. He is with
God, confronted and prevented and elected and summoned by [God]."[61] There
follow sixty-six pages of repetitious but often powerful and profound interpretation of human freedom, responsibility, historicity, and other themes. Once we
know the basis for understanding the real human, we can reconsider the entire
discussion of the phenomenal human.

Barth again reminds the reader that he did not deny or repudiate the phenomena of the human; they merely give a portrait of a shadow. But once we
know the real, those aspects of the phenomenal human can be estimated as
"real *indications*" of the human" (italics added). It can now be affirmed "that all
scientific knowledge of man is not objectively empty, but has a real object."[62] All
human self-knowledge, even though it assumes human autonomy, is justifiable
as *real symptoms* of the human. But "[t]he being of man cannot be explained
from these symptoms." The main point of the critique "was simply to refute the

claim that it could be genuine knowledge of a real object independently of a prior knowledge of real man."[63]

What Barth takes away—that is, confidence that secular knowledge, whether scientific, ethical, existential, or theistic, discloses the truly human— he now gives back to be interpreted theologically. This is a distinctive accom- modation position of the relation of secular to theological disciplines. They are not rejected, per se, nor are they the basis for a theology. Rather, at least in gen- eral, they are accepted within their limits, and then reinterpreted christologi- cally. Secular disciplines disclose that humans are *capable* of being in the history of a gracious election. "*Capacity* for this being is the essence of all forms and symptoms of the human" (italics added).[64] From the standpoint of knowledge of the being of the human, the phenomena accounted for by secular disciplines show the capacity, endowment, and adaptability of humans. They are elements of the *potentiality* that is actualized in being. God created humans with this ca- pacity. Secular disciplines do not give knowledge of our being, but they give more or less exact knowledge of our *capacity* to be human. They do not give knowledge of our reality, but do give more or less comprehensive knowledge of our *possibility*.

Thus, retrospectively, "[w]hat natural science sees and tries to understand and present as man may certainly be a symptom" of true human nature. The same is true for the ethical interpretation, existentialist philosophy, and theism. Indeed, "a knowledge of man which is non-theological but genuine is not only possible but basically justified and *necessary* even from the standpoint of theo- logical anthropology" (italics added). The source of this knowledge is not the Word and revelation of God, but "this does not necessarily mean that what it knows . . . is false or worthless." "Theological anthropology is prepared to wel- come all such general knowledge of [the human]."[65]

Yes, theological anthropology is prepared to welcome general knowledge of the human. But the sciences of the human, or any other, for Barth are of no significance for what is distinctive about the human per se. Because knowl- edge of God is given in the Bible, a gracious God known in Jesus, the doctrine of God is immune from any criticism, alteration, restriction, or other correc- tion from secular scholarship. The real human is understood in relational terms, that is, as determined by God's action in Jesus. It is related to the divine initiative by being summoned, obedient, and responsible to God. Thus only in an oblique way, if at all, does the descriptive axiom of this book hold for Barth. Yes, the same phenomenon, the human, is addressed or accounted for by both secular disciplines and theology. But Barth's radical disjuncture between the phenomenal human and the real human *implies that the sciences and theology are not addressing exactly the same reality*. The sciences, ethics, and existential phi- losophy address the phenomenal; theology addresses the real. The only signifi- cant intersection in Barth's theological anthropology is that the secular disciplines account for a capacity, a possibility, a potentiality for humans to know their relation to God.

Barth does not, in the passage I have analyzed, refer to any social scientific accounts of religion and human action that are central to Milbank's argument. It is logical to infer, however, that if social and behavioral sciences disclosed aspects of the phenomenal human they would also explain the capacity and possibility for relationship with God. While Barth is critical of any use for the sciences that assumes their sufficiency, he does not engage in a diatribe against "the Enlightenment project," as do Milbank and Hauerwas and Ochs. His is far from the option of rejecting secular disciplines. Yet as seems to be the case in those "postmodern" sources, so also for Barth theology is an *autonomous* discipline. Its source, content, and procedures are based on revealed knowledge. Thus, in any intersection with secular disciplines the theological disciplines flow in one direction. Traffic from others comes in from side roads to be directed by theology.[66]

Barth would certainly reject Hefner's project, which uses biology not to show a capacity for relationship to God but to interpret the activity of God through nature. In *The Human Factor* Hefner's theology is basically one of the first articles of the creed: creation. Barth's, as the late Swedish theologian Gustaf Wingren often argued, is a theology of the second article: Christ. No inferences from scientific accounts of nature can be used to expound the core of Christian theology: God's election of humans is in and through Jesus alone.

There is an affinity between Farley's and Barth's work at one juncture, namely, biology and the capacity to relate to an "other" are both aspects of the human. Farley, like Barth, explains a capacity and possibility for redemption from secular sources. But Farley desires to overcome the radical disjuncture between the phenomenal and real human. For him, this is an example of the "ghost of Mani," as if the real human is "something floating above nature and the body." Indeed, Farley might argue that Barth proposes a dualism that avoids but does not overcome cognitive dissonance. Secular disciplines account for the phenomenal aspects, theology accounts for the real aspects. But theology subsumes the secular in a reinterpretation made on the authority of revealed knowledge.

Not only theology but also theological ethics is an autonomous discipline for Barth. An analysis of his ethics, parallel to that of the human, can be made from his extended expositions in *Church Dogmatics* II/2 and III/4. The basic moves are similar. Ethics is sin if it assumes that a person, not God, has the prerogative of determining what is right and good. Casuistry, the rational application of moral principles to cases, usurps the divine prerogative; it makes human reason the final arbiter of the morally correct. Secular ethics and law are similar to the phenomenal human; they claim self-sufficiency. Christian ethics is based on the command of the gracious God known in Jesus. Once the difference is known, and it is understood that persons are to hear the command of God in specific circumstances, the law becomes the form of the gospel, and practical casuistry gives points to be considered in preparing to hear a specific command of God. Sciences also help to understand the occasions in which God is commanding but they do not determine God's decision. No secular disciplines can alter Barth's theology and ethics, based as they are on God's election of the human in Jesus.[67]

Theologians, moral theologians, and pastors find a fundamental coherence and persuasiveness in Barth's theology and ethics, once its suppositions are granted. This book, however, invites them into a different context, that in which my fictive college student moves from course to course in neuroscience, Kantian moral philosophy, cultural anthropology, economics, molecular chemistry, and religious studies—and also reads Aeschylus, Shakespeare, and Toni Morrison. A descriptive axiom of this book is that most persons in our culture, both within and outside the churches, understand the human, and other phenomena that are addressed in religious discourse, in secular terms. If this is the case, would saying that "whatever else a human being is, she is with Jesus and therefore with God" be persuasive, or even intelligible, to the student? In cross-disciplinary seminars of faculty from all parts of a university, could one make intelligible the proposition that only in Christian theology is the *real* human fully known? A case could be made that a capacity for wonder is grounded in human nature, but in a religiously plural and mostly secularized group of scholars, can one claim that to be human is to have the man Jesus as a "Kinsman, Neighbour and Brother"?

Can the modern world be absorbed into the biblical view, as George Lindbeck commends in his influential *The Nature of Doctrine*?[68] In one sense Barth has absorbed the sciences into his distinctive version of the biblical view. But the biblical view is immune to what is absorbed into it. The biblical theologians I know do not use biblical language as their mother tongue when speaking about political events, mental illness, and the economy. Few members of churches would use Barth's vocabulary to claim that the reality of their humanity is their divine determination by God's grace made known in the man Jesus. This would probably be the last thing that would come to mind when confronted by a political choice, symptoms of a debilitating and fatal disease, poverty and social chaos in cities around the world, their Jewish, Hindu, and Muslim neighbors, not to mention their radically secularized children and grandchildren.

Barth seems to overcome cognitive dissonance when the knowledge of the phenomenal human is credited with the capacity and potentiality to know the Divine. But it is autonomous theology that correctly assesses what is described and explained by the secular sciences. Meaning is drawn from a unique authoritative source.

These theological writings, which explicitly attend to the relation of secular knowledge of the human to theology and other religious discourse, are intellectually sophisticated. Only those that opt for rejection clearly resolve the issues, though in a way that avoids rather than confronts the issues of this book. Theological traffic goes its own way, and secular its own way. Even Hefner's book, which appears to make the secular traffic determine the flow of theology, never permits that completely. Both Hefner and Farley want to overcome the "ghost of Mani," a radical dualism, but some things about the human evade full explanation by the sciences alone. Thus tension, if not dualism, continues to lurk. Barth's position is unique: the first stance is rejection, though always qualified. But the rejection is based on God's particular revelation in Jesus. If dualism is overcome, it is by permitting traffic from secular studies to be controlled by theology.

What sophisticated theologians cannot agree on is something all religious persons, willy-nilly, confront where the secular discourses of our culture meet their religious beliefs and activities. This historical concern of liberal theology can be suppressed, ignored, or verbally bypassed, but it will not disappear.

4

The Importance of Contexts

The focus of the previous chapters was academic. By using the human as an extended example of an intersection, they showed theologians consciously and deliberately relating secular and religious discourse by directing traffic in different ways. Different examples could have been used to illustrate the existence of other unavoidable intersections, for example, scientific cosmology and the doctrine of creation. Intersections exist in every possible example. The flow of traffic across them upholds the primary descriptive axiom of this book: the same events, actions, and texts that are addressed by theology and ethics are also addressed by other academic disciplines. Moreover, the ideal-types of response—rejection, absorption, and accommodation—help to analyze the differences among theologians.

This chapter does not neglect the academic context of theological and scientific ideas, but explores the social and other contexts of not only academics but also religious persons, groups, and institutions. Theological and scientific ideas emerge in more immediate and often practical contexts. My simple typology also illumines relations to them.[1]

The significance of scientific and other secular interpretations for religious beliefs and activities is always *relational*. Significant for whom? An academic theologian in a university? A metaphysician? A pastor immersed in the details of the life of a congregation and community? A layperson trying to resolve ambiguities in her personal religious beliefs? Significant for what? To defend the distinctive rigor of Christian ethics? To protect the historical identity and integrity of orthodox Christians doctrines? To maintain the unique identity of the church? To attract secular person to the Christian community by showing affinity between their senses of the divine and moral responsibility and Christian faith and life? Or, on the part of skeptics, to debunk religion in the light of the sciences? The significance is related to many interests that theologians, pastors, and other Christians, as well as some secular persons, have.

The significance is relative to the *theological* or *faith* dispositions and commitments of persons, groups, and institutions. Unitarians, seeking maximum coherence between science and religion, come to the intersection differently from churches that require adherence to biblical literalism or historic creeds. In interreligious dialogues Hindus, Buddhists, and Muslims meet relevant secular knowledge at different places from Christians and Jews, and interests differ among members of each group. A Muslim fundamentalist rejects; a Muslim rationalist accommodates.

The significance is relative to the *moral* commitments and human values of persons, groups, and institutions. Christian liberationists and members of the Christian Coalition respond to the same scientific interpretations differently. For the former, biological and psychological explanations of homophilia lead to compassionate understanding and respect, and inclusion of gays and lesbians in the church. For the latter, they do not mitigate moral condemnation; exclusion from the church is required.

The significance varies from one *social* and *cultural* location to another. The Christian dalits in India and educated Canadian Christians bring their religious queries from incomparable social and cultural backgrounds. Second-generation Korean Christians in the United States have a different perspective from their grandparents in Korea.

The significance is also relative to personal and social *experiences*. Innocent victims of debilitating and painful diseases or natural disasters explained by the sciences might discard their confidence in God's love for them. Others, believing that their circumstances are divine retribution, might be relieved by scientific explanations. Some might find consolation and hope in God's love for them in spite of scientific explanations of cancer and tornadoes. Families that have lived in poverty generation after generation might find it hard to believe that God prefers the poor.[2]

This chapter focuses on the contexts that inform the flow of traffic, including those of the theologians analyzed above, and thus uses a different descriptive axiom. Most readers—theologians, pastors, or laypersons—have either tacitly or consciously altered or abandoned some traditional beliefs and practices in light of scientific or other secular interpretations of human life, of natural and historical events, and of society and culture. The intersection of traffic is not just *out there*; it is also *in us*.

Surely for most Christian groups and individuals, whether theologians or laypersons, these four factors are background conditions that, in interaction with one another, shape how religious and secular interpretations are related. And surely there is little self-critical awareness of their influence. It is instructive in reading Christian religious discourse to ask some critical questions.

What seems to worry an author or preacher? What is she trying to protect against damaging criticism? What is he trying to endorse and why? Anxieties and commitments orient persons and groups toward particular intersections of religious and secular discourse.

The interests and outlooks of no human beings are exclusively defined by the sciences, or religious and moral commitments and beliefs, or political, economic, and familial experiences. The issues are not only intellectual and academic. They are *in us* as persons, groups, and institutions, as well as *out there* in university seminars, learned society meetings, and scholarly books. Historic group experiences (sometimes called "collective memory") such as slavery or the Holocaust shape outlooks and choices more profoundly than theological ideas. One difference between our time and that of Jonathan Edwards and John Calvin is the unavoidable exposure to many more alternative descriptions, explanations, valuations, and meanings of actions and events. Movies, dramas, television entertainment and talk shows, novels, printed commentaries, and art influence far more people than sermons and theological treatises. They affect emotions and desires as well as thinking. Effective media presentations shape goals and aspirations, loves and hates, and immediate gratifications in ways that seldom come under self-conscious scrutiny. The pace of technological and cultural change is exponentially faster than in the eighteenth and sixteenth centuries. The responses of persons to a collapsing church gallery, or insufficient lactation, can be interpreted from many more alternative perspectives. All persons, not only theologians and other Christians, *value different interpretations* of the same events and actions. All have multiple experiences, interests, beliefs, commitments, and objectives.

Few, if any, have a hierarchical order that predetermines every action and response. Few first ask what religious beliefs ought to direct their activities. Few first ask how the love commandment should apply to particular choices and actions. Few, if any, theologians, pastors, or laypeople determine the course of their lives by a designed Christian rational life plan, or in "disinterested" intellectual isolation. Only some theologians are focused on the logical compatibility or incompatibility of abstract theological concepts with abstract metaphysical or scientific ideas. Rather, an *interaction* occurs in which religious loyalties, personal anxieties, contemporary and historical concerns, and other nondoctrinal factors intersect with particular scientific and other secular interpretations and with the perceived ethos of their times and places. Positions are shaped in interaction between ideas—theological and secular interpretations of the same phenomena—and personal and group experiences, historical and cultural contexts, and religious concerns of interpreters.[3]

Theologians who are interested primarily in justifying religious beliefs intersect with epistemologists and philosophers of science. Important traditional issues are addressed, for example, realism, relativism, and efforts to

avoid radicalized extremes of either. The historical distinction between natural
and revealed theology, and the relations between them, continue to be discussed. A philosophy of religion has to be settled prior to interpreting Christian doctrines. Primary attention is given to theological method, and hundreds
of articles and books address it.[4]

Secular counterparts for decades in North America were Anglo-American
philosophers of language and historians and philosophers of science. Not long
after Thomas Kuhn's *Structure of Scientific Revolutions* was published it was cited
by theologians, sometimes to mitigate the authority of the sciences and thus
deflect some criticism of theology. Wittgenstein's writings from various times
in his career were used by some philosophers of religion and theologians. They
warranted, for some Christians, distinctions between different "language
games," for example, the language of science and the language of religion. Religious language and scientific language are incommensurable. Attacks on "pos-
itivism" gave comfort to some theologians. Narrative became authentic
religious discourse. Others attended more to phenomenology and hermeneutics. Often what is currently in vogue in secular academic discourse attracts interest, for example, "postmodernism."[5] Theologians want to be au courant with
intellectual trends that drive other scholars.

In a similar way many theological ethicists, impressed by the lack of intellectual rigor in much Protestant literature, turned to secular counterparts in
moral philosophy. Whereas an earlier generation drew from idealism, a new
one drew from the analysis of moral language, and especially the "is-ought" distinction, and arguments between deontologists and consequentialists, and
other historical and contemporary sources. Ethical methodology and theory
became foci of attention among theologians just as they were among philosophers. The Bible was examined to see if it backed deontological, teleological, or
virtue ethics. Moral philosophers provided analytic procedures for clarifying
formal issues in theological and social ethics. Theologians, taking a cue from
philosopher William Frankena, distinguished between "act-agapism" and "rule-
agapism." Christian love is which? Moral theologians, like systematic theologians, argued with one another about methodology. Concern for ethical theory
became more significant than how ethics is related to theology, moral life to religious life, and Christology to ethics. Methodological issues had to be settled
before addressing theological and practical ethics. Some authors debated the
merits of especially important books, such as John Rawls's *Theory of Justice* and
Alisdair MacIntyre's *After Virtue,* before they went on to address questions of
social justice and Christian virtue. Moral theologians also like to be au courant
with intellectual trends of their secular counterparts.[6]

If a theologian's focus is on the Christian doctrine of creation, her work will
intersect with scientific interpretations of the origin of the universe, the evolution of living organisms, the ordering of nature, and its projected ends (*telos* and

finis). She might find herself engaged in the publications of astrophysicist Steven Weinberg, evolutionary theorist Ernst Mayr, and books by scientists that venture speculations, such as Theodosius Dobzhansky's *Mankind Evolving* and Freeman Dyson's *Infinite in All Directions*. Like Jürgen Moltmann, she might cite theories of an open universe to corroborate her eschatology. But hypotheses about the demise of our planet and its life could raise serious questions about traditional Christian language about the future. Creation by the Word of God does not easily cohere with secular theories of the origin of the universe. There will be, at least, tensions between the impersonal ordering of nature, which can be taken as divine governance, and God as person—a personal, intentional, active agent—who is concerned primarily with human well-being and who, like a mother, loves each child. The tensions, present in much of historical theology, are more complex in light of the natural sciences.[7]

A Christian theologian's preference for a particular ethical theory affects how he assimilates, or rejects, secular accounts of events and actions, as well as his moral judgments and prescribed course of action. If he is a theological utilitarian, believing that the purpose of Christian love is to maximize the human good and minimize the evil, secular knowledge will provide the content of outcomes of interventions into interpersonal, historical, or natural processes. He judges which are good on the basis of Christian love. If he is a deontologist, his theologically authorized ethical principles and rules are plumb lines to judge secular accounts of circumstances and actions. If his theological belief is that God acts in natural and historical events, the first question is, What is God doing? An answer requires a direct religious and moral interpretation of secular, often scientific, accounts.

A moral theologian concerned about environmental problems might be satisfied only to articulate a biblical outlook that sees humans as stewards, not possessors, of nature. Or, she might challenge the technological ethos for its utilitarian and anthropocentric trajectory that spurs the exploitation of nature. Nature is "commodified" (in Max Weber's terms, "thingified") rather than respected or revered. She might find in the poetry of Goethe, Wordsworth, and Tennyson an affinity with her Christian outlook. Asian religious traditions might attract her, with their symbols of nature as an organic whole that decenters the "Western" view of the human. But if the theologian wishes to make particular policy recommendations about the disposal of nuclear waste or global warming, he intersects with the research of ecological scientists, economists' accounts of cost-benefit analyses, and both domestic and international political powers. Faced with different analyses of present and future circumstances, the theologian has to assess secular explanations of environmental problems. He has to question whether his preference for one or the other is based on its scientific reliability or his moral outlook. An aesthetic rather than mechanistic approach to nature might be religiously preferable, but institutionalized

economic, legal, and political forces make the biggest difference. Consumer behavior should be tempered by Christian asceticism, but this has limited effect
on governments and corporations.

The globalization of the market economy, with its ensuing discrepancies
between rich and poor, will anger a theologian or pastor whose sense of injustice is based on God's will for justice. To make cogent judgments and recommendations, however, she has to evaluate historical, economic, political, and
cultural explanations of conditions she finds unjust, and she has to decide
which features from each will be combined in a theological ethical interpretation. Descriptions and explanations of circumstances in India and Mexico, in
Silicon Valley and Gastonia, North Carolina, necessarily differ. Religious and
moral discourse are not sufficient to determine which scholarly accounts are
most reliable, whatever ideas of love and justice are held dear. Arguments may
be about descriptions and explanations, not about God's action or moral principles and ethical theory. To observe that value preferences affect secular studies does not warrant their dismissal. Intersection with them is a decisive aspect
of practical social ethics and moral theology.

Many examples can be cited to demonstrate that social and cultural factors
and group experiences are contexts from which religious discourse intersects
with scientific and other secular discourse. The social context and experiences
of minorities, as we have seen for decades, is a consciously defined standpoint
for religious thinking. Historians, sociologists, novelists, and others contribute
to an understanding of minority status and experience. The persuasiveness of a
black theologian depends, in part, on his interpretation of the historical, social,
economic, and political circumstances of African American groups and individuals. The effect on a reader comes not only from the use of biblical narratives
and theology, but also from the authenticity of the account of minority experiences. Since secular analyses differ, a critical theologian, like an environmental
ethicist, assesses them for their scholarly merit as well as for their compatibility with his religious outlook.

Feminist religious thought is as compelling as black theology. Collective
and individual experiences of oppressive restrictions are the context from
which traditional theology and ethics are addressed. Biological, historical, psychological, social scientific, and literary scholarship contributes to the interpretation. Arguments of feminist theologians are more persuasive for their
incisive interpretations of women's experiences than for their use of traditional
doctrines. Women's experiences are the intersection. A coherent description,
evaluation, and meaning of them evoke a religious and moral critique of cus-
tomary Christian thinking and acting, and reorient theology and ethics. Theologians have to assess arguments among secular scholars. Differences in
women's theology stem, in part, from preferences for different secular accounts. For example, should women's uniqueness be considered more impor-

tant than their "equality" with men? Religious sources alone cannot settle the answer.

The religious and moral discourse that most deeply affects the lives and thinking of pastors and laypeople addresses their contexts and experiences. These are illumined more by secular interpretations than by any that confine themselves to traditional religious symbols and narratives.[8]

Inferences to Be Drawn

To keep manageable control over the variety of interests and contexts, a return to the theologians analyzed in the previous chapter in light of the descriptive axiom of this one is instructive. What contexts—religious and theological, moral, social and cultural, and experiential—have affected their basic stances and their rejections or accommodations? What religious, theological, and moral anxieties determine what traffic they direct, and how? Contexts are quite clear and specific in some cases; inferences have to be drawn in others. A hypothetical and suggestive, rather than exhaustive and detailed, account is sufficient. In the case of Barth many studies, including biographies, have related events in his historical context to his theology; not even a summary of them is attempted here. Each author assumes a context from which he works, and to which he addresses his arguments.

Milbank and Hauerwas and Ochs, whose work tends toward, or even endorses, rejection of the applicability of scientific knowledge to theology, shape their interpretations in response to many other factors and not only on the authority of the Bible and tradition. Interaction occurs between "modernity" and theology and ethics. Their positions are responses to their descriptions and explanations of the intellectual climate they fault. Their persuasiveness depends on a reader's acceptance of their interpretation of how contemporary culture affects Christianity. One infers that this context threatens the uniqueness and integrity of Christian theology, the distinctiveness of Christian ethics, and the historical identity of the Christian church. The Zeitgeist requires a clear proclamation of the uniqueness of Christian beliefs and practices. The radical particularity of Christian beliefs and morality that they endorse is plausibly provoked by their passionate hostility to "modernity" and "the Enlightenment project." One wonders if they would prefer to have lived before the Enlightenment: in societies where inherited social status determined possibilities of individual achievement, where there was no political democracy, where rights were conferred by heteronomous authority rather than human equality, where serfdom and slavery were accepted, where the freedom of scholarly inquiry was restricted by religious dogma, where religious freedom was restricted by concordats between church and state, and so on. Their case against absorption and accommodation requires a compelling account of threats against it, not just the assertion of a radical orthodoxy and narrative theology, though each reinforces the others.

The processes by which the identity of Christianity persists through time are social, historical, and cultural. In many respects they are the same as those that sustain the distinctiveness of the Daughters of the Confederacy, the Masonic order, the National Rifle Association, and the Swedish Social Democratic Party. Memories of decisive events are rehearsed; specific symbols, narratives, concepts, and practices reinforce a sense of belonging to each group, and its stance toward the world. Belief that God chose to be revealed uniquely, absolutely, and finally in Jesus and the Bible does not explain Christianity's historical distinctiveness. Secular explanation of it as a social movement is needed.

From Hefner's book one infers that he has a strong conviction about the current intellectual context of religion and theology. Biology, in both evolutionary and molecular terms, has two profound influences. First, it provides a comprehensive explanation of human life in the evolving universe. Like theology, its concepts describe, explain, evaluate, and give meaning to life. This is the case for some persons. It can be distinguished from other academic disciplines that also influence the way humans think and act. For example, a Freudian perspective functions for some persons in a similar way. In the mid-twentieth century theologians Paul Tillich and David Roberts accommodated to it. Marxism also provides a comprehensive explanation of history, politics, and society. For many theologians it has been more significant than Darwinism. Either because Hefner is engaged in the dialogue between science and theology, or because he judges biology's influence to be very deep and broad, it takes precedence over economics, psychology, and humanistic studies.

The second influence is from Hefner's confidence in the explanatory power of the biological sciences, both macroscopically in evolutionary terms and microscopically in molecular terms. He knows that sciences have histories and develop through time, but this does not necessarily relativize the reliability of current research. Traditional theology has to take account of them, since they both interpret the same phenomena. Unlike E. O. Wilson and Richard Dawkins, the Christian Hefner does not use them to debunk religious beliefs and morality. Rather, he moves toward absorption of biology into theology, an accommodation that leans to the left. Traffic from it strongly determines the theological course.

Just as the persuasiveness of Milbank and Hauerwas and Ochs depends on a reader's assessment of their cultural analysis, Hefner's persuasiveness depends on how one judges his conviction about the importance and the influence of biology. Or, it might be that his apologetic is directed toward his peers in the science and theology discussions. He seeks extensive compatibility between science and theology. Persons who use biological evidences to alter more specific judgments, for example, against homophilia, must be circumspect in their critiques of Hefner. Although the intersection is more central to his theology, in both cases sciences require a rerouting of religious and moral traffic.

Farley, like Hefner, responds to the profound influence of the sciences on our understanding of the human. In the context of a scientifically influenced culture he is deeply concerned about the credibility, or at least intelligibility, of Christian theology. Biological sciences require accommodation by theology, even if radical reinterpretation is the outcome. Farley's account, however, is more complex than Hefner's. The experience of freedom, intentionality, and intersubjectivity is also part of human life. He has a deeper conviction that these experiences cannot be explained by the sciences. Thus he adduces descriptions by European phenomenologists, especially Emmanuel Levinas. He argues that biology establishes more than necessary conditions for full human experience; it eliminates the ghost of Mani. Even so, philosophy accounts for what biology cannot explain. The radical dualism between body and spirit in the Christian tradition is presumably overcome by melding scientific explanations and philosophical descriptions into the flow of his philosophical anthropology. His subsequent theological exposition of good and evil is compatible with this interpretation.

Biological determinists, however, would find Farley to be incoherent since the scientific explanations are not carried to their logical conclusions, even if current research has not explained the experiences of freedom, intentionality, and intersubjectivity. Farley acknowledges the limits of the sciences; he would judge Hefner to have conceded too much. Barth, however, would judge even Farley to have given too much credence to the explanatory powers of secular sources. They cannot account for the "real man."

Both Hefner's and Farley's persuasiveness depends on agreement with their understanding of how deeply the sciences influence current understandings of the human. Like Schleiermacher, Troeltsch, and others, Hefner and Farley believe that in the context of modern culture the implications of the sciences for theology must be forthrightly confronted. Radical disjuncture between them has to be overcome, or at least modified. Some pattern of continuity with the sciences is required for contemporary Christians. The trajectory of classic liberal Protestant theology cannot be deflected: "modernity" will not go away. Farley's interpretation of the human is in that trajectory; it establishes the parameters within which contemporary theology and ethics are expounded. For Farley, it is too strong to claim that the meaning of the sciences is *transformed* by theology. It is also incorrect to claim that theology provides the true, or deeper, meaning of the secular. But Farley does want Christians out of the box of double truths in which science and theology are each valid in their own sphere, but never meet. Farley uses metaphors rather than causal arguments to relate the two. The sciences and theology should flow together in some way; each should not take a different fork in the road when they meet. Biological determinists, as well as others, might also argue that Farley has not expelled the ghost of Mani.

But neither have other theologians who accommodate to the sciences.

The modern cultural complex in which Christian theologians, pastors, and laypeople live and think is also part of Barth's context. Indeed, secular patterns of thought have hegemony in modern society. Barth, however, gives more autonomy to theology than do Hefner and Farley. The mission and ministry of the church are the primary context. His conviction that the *true* knowledge of "*real* man" is found only in the Bible is radically different from Hefner's and Farley's. Secular sources are not false per se, but become false when they claim to know the real human. And they are falsely relied upon when knowledge of God is based on them. Hefner and Farley would agree to a point, but Barth's argument for the inadequacy of secular knowledge is grounded in his Christology. Unlike Milbank, however, he does not fault "modernity" as a cultural epoch. Readers have to be persuaded that his accounts of both revealed theology and secular sources are sound. It is the former that warrants the limited significance of the latter. Secular sources give knowledge only of the phenomenal human. By denying Barth's sharp distinction between the real and the phenomenal, Hefner and Farley grant more authority to the sciences. Barth's interpretation of them is always in a mirror; what they reliably show is reflected off his Christology. Only when the truly human is known in Jesus can their important, but subordinate, role be properly understood.

The radical distinction between the phenomenal and the real continues a long history of dualism in Christian theology and Western philosophy. Most contemporary theologians known to me argue neither for physical determinism nor for the spirit hovering over the body. Some find biblical precedent for this. Most, tacitly or explicitly, are responding to the extensive influence of the sciences. Various linguistic devices and concepts are used to attempt to put both the ghost of Mani and "biologism" or "scientism" to rest. Farley writes that humans and animals have the same "condition." "Self-presencing" is not a physiological state, but occurs "in conjunction with a living organism." "[T]he biological dimension of agents does not occur prior to or even along side of [freedom, love, and intersubjectivity] but pervades and influences them."[9] One can argue that Barth's return to the characteristics of "phenomenal man" approximates Farley's position. But Farley's use of Levinas describes only one stage of Barth's "phenomenal man." Milbank rejects any causal implications of Farley's or Hefner's terms: "Theology can evade all and every social [and by implication natural] scientific suspicion, and history is its ally: written history, which produces exceptions to the supposed universal rule; lived history which permits us always to enact the different."[10] To Hefner and Farley, this judgment consigns Christians to extreme cognitive dissonance. Dissonance is mitigated in the realm of ideas by rejecting any implications for theology from the sciences. It is harder to mitigate it in lived experience.

Theologians, pastors, and laypeople inevitably live and think in our scientifically informed culture. It is their daily milieu. Contemporary Christians can absorb, reject, or accommodate. Some live and think without critical self-awareness, moving easily from realm to realm as situations emerge. Some have found security in the absolute authority of the Bible and historic creeds, or the church. Some leave the church and find security only by replacing Christian dogmatism with secular dogmatism. But many "mainstream" Protestants, liberal Catholics, and even evangelicals are at least aware of dissonance. What is called "unapologetic theology" attempts to suppress the religious importance of this condition; it becomes discourse internal to the church.

Contemporary debates in Christian theology and ethics are often about which context ought to be determinative. Arguments that the church is the proper and limited context currently flourish. For one radical trajectory the scientific cultural context is there, but its hegemony is that which theology is defined against. Christian ethics becomes ethics for Christians by refusing to incorporate ethics derived from secular sources. The classic liberal tradition of Schleiermacher, Troeltsch, and others accepted the necessity of explicit and reasoned accommodation of Christian thinking and life to scientific and other secular knowledge. The weight of this book is on their side for intellectual and academic reasons, for social and cultural reasons, and because Christian individuals can seek to suppress, but cannot avoid being shaped by, "modernity."

Recall previous chapters of this book. Each of the theologians discussed in earlier chapters is, in some way, answering the questions I raised about Edwards's account of the collapse of the gallery, and Calvin's account of lactation. And so do others. Has a theologian accepted a naturalistic, scientific account, and then reinterpreted it theologically? Barth, maybe. Has the scientific account substantially altered the meaning of the theological account? Hefner, maybe. Does the scientific account have no importance for the theological account? Milbank and Hauerwas and Ochs, maybe. Do two accounts, scientific and philosophical, complement each other, and then become the basis for theological interpretation? Farley, maybe. Every theologian, pastor, and Christian believer in our culture either tacitly or explicitly answers those questions, at least vaguely. Historical relativism, diversity of religious traditions, and the development of the sciences ("modernity") will not evaporate. The religious issue is how this context will be taken into account in Christian beliefs, morals, and actions.

Navigating the Intersections

The Light of Truth

The previous chapters have been pedagogical, showing ways to analyze Christian theology and ethics that address the primary descriptive axiom of the book: the same actions, events, texts, and other phenomena that religious discourse addresses are also accounted for by other disciplines. Theology and the sciences intersect, for example, in the human; religious and secular accounts meet. The first part of this chapter lifts out for more specific attention the distinctions that have been used; they are commended here as heuristic devices that can be used more widely.

The primarily pedagogical sections have also been critical of some of the alternative positions. Critical comments have highlighted their distinctiveness in a comparative way. But they have also disclosed my standpoint: The agenda of classic liberal Protestant theology is not superseded by subsequent theological fashions, though its constructive proposals are inadequate.[1] Christian life and thought exist in a context in which historical and cultural relativism are deeply embedded; in which other historical religious traditions and secularism are materials not only to be addressed intellectually, but also in our personal experience and that of our neighbors and our families; in which various sciences interpret nature, events, and experiences that are present in religious thought and life. Thus the second part of this chapter is frankly polemical and hortatory; it makes a case for my standpoint for contemporary Christian theology, ethics, preaching, and pastoral care, and for self-examination of Christian life and community.

Locating Differences in Interpretation: Description, Explanation, Evaluation, and Meaning

Interaction is inevitable among religious, academic, and other secular discourse. Even Christian discourse that attempts to avoid being tainted by secular scholarship defines itself against traffic that inevitably comes toward it at intersections such as biblical texts, the human, the physical universe, and so on. Theologically driven "creation science" that seeks to make the Genesis account credible not only believes in its historical accuracy but also argues against scientific evolutionary theory. We are not often conscious of what we absorb that modifies our religious and ethical views, or what we deflect to avoid confrontations. Even when there is awareness of the content and processes of interaction, secular influences can be deliberately ignored or even suppressed. Probably every Christian theologian, pastor, and layperson lives with some degree of cognitive dissonance. So also do others whose outlook is affected by intellectual and cultural currents that cannot be melded into a smooth flow. This book has a pedagogical and critical objective to raise self-awareness of Christians about the merging of traffic in their writing, speaking, and living.

The first chapter shows that the interpretation of intersections has several dimensions, for which I have used the terms *description, explanation, valuation, and meaning.* These terms are distinguished to aid in locating more differences in interpretations. The materials to which they refer flow into each other in the processes of interpretation and understanding; they are not discrete activities that sequentially follow each other beginning with either description or meaning. A comprehensive framework of the meaning of actions and events affects which aspects are most significant and valued most; thus it also affects the description and explanation. A particular description of an event or action orients an explanation of it; the explanation affects the description, in part on the basis of the evaluations of the significance of factors, and even a preferred large framework of meaning.[2] The boundaries are porous, and the flow varies with individuals and communities. Indeed, different disciplines, or scholars within a discipline, focus on one or two more than others. Sometimes different perspectives and disciplinary research methods account for the same phenomena in such different ways that one wonders if the same action or event is being interpreted. Some political scientists focus on describing, quantifying, and evaluating factors that yield the most comprehensive and accurate "scientific" explanation of events. Others, such as "realists" in international relations, are predisposed to interpret events in the light of that major perspective which history has taught them. Certain critical events in various spheres become powerful metaphors to express the meaning of other events. My colleagues and I once examined "Vietnam" as a metaphor to illumine other political situations, and "Tuskegee" (immoral use of subjects in syphilis research) as a metaphor that makes African Americans wary of other publicly funded health-care experiments. "Exodus" functions similarly in some theological discourse, as does "crucifixion/resurrection." They become religious metaphors that interpret the meaning of historical and personal events. But it is useful to distinguish among these four terms when analyzing differences of interpretation of the same action, events, or other phenomena.

I described how an economist and a cultural anthropologist interpret the potlatch ceremony of Native Americans differently. They can agree on a minimal description of a process of exchange. Beyond that their disciplinary perspectives penetrate interpretations. The utility value of the goods exchanged is more important for the economist than the cultural meaning of the transaction preferred by the anthropologist. Preferred explanations thus affect the importance of different aspects of what can be agreed upon in a minimal description. Their different interpretations verify their disciplinary perspectives in a nonvicious circular way. The amateur reader of the controversy perceives that traffic turns in different directions when the scholars meet. Are arguments about descriptions? The anthropologist will include things in her description that are not important to the economist. Are they about explanations? The anthropologist explains the ceremony by its symbolic meanings for the participants; the economist, by the utility value of exchanges. Are they about evaluations? Each judges the importance of aspects of the exchange differently. Are they about meaning? Verification of research is found in the concepts and argumentation characteristic of each one's disciplinary perspective.[3]

The naming of a course of events predisposes persons to describe, explain, evaluate, and give different meanings to them. During the Vietnam War, ethical discussion and political communication were very difficult because of passions, but also because parties finally named the war differently. To some it was a war against Communism; to others it was a war of liberation against Western domination and oppression. A minimal descriptive account of events might be agreed upon, though there was suspicion about the accuracy of facts. The names implied different explanations of the causes and justifications of the war. Different events and information were evaluated differently. The meanings implied by the names were relative to political interests and loyalties, but also to moral outlooks. Which is the evil to be overcome? Anyone attempting to moderate an argument from a relatively disinterested academic perspective found that the different political and moral perspectives implied in the names was the ultimate barrier against rational analysis.

Even the best intention to arrive at less dissonance is frustrated, whether between religious and secular accounts or different disciplinary accounts. During the Cold War physicist Robert Sachs, a former director of Argonne National Laboratories, and I conducted a seminar of faculty members from various institutions in the Chicago metropolitan area on the ethics of nuclear deterrence. Participants were physicists, chemists, Sovietologists, experts on conventional weapons, political scientists, historians, literary critics, philosophers and theologians, and others. It was provisionally agreed that nuclear war could not be morally justified. The more refined question was: if it is immoral to use nuclear weapons, is it immoral to threaten to use them? In the many months we met, MAD (mutually assured destruction) was the major fact of international affairs. Papers by various participants were read and discussed; conscientious efforts were made to comprehend the varied contributions. The session that terminated the seminar was led by a Kantian moral philosopher. With impeccable logic from his ethical theory he proved that if it was immoral to use nuclear weapons, it was immoral to threaten to use them. It takes no imagination to see how this was responded to by an expert on nuclear and conventional weaponry in place in central and eastern Europe, by a military strategist for whom the Kola Peninsula was a more important place in Europe than Florence or Paris, and others. The traffic of a logically impeccable ethical argument never met the traffic of political scientists, military strategists, and others. The ethical stance purposely located the moral factor as decisive. To some participants from other fields the implications were "out of this world." The philosopher conceded that his argument had logical military and political consequences that he could not fully endorse, which only proved to others the irrelevance of purely ethical arguments.[4]

The basic agenda of this book is not limited to intersections of religious and secular discourse, but pervades historical, political, and social analyses to which just about everyone is exposed in newscasts and magazines of commentary, if not in scholarly literature. Commentators on an economic slump cite not only the competitive free market, but also psychological conditions that influence investors and consumers. Pundits who analyze international crises and violence include not only military and political forces, but also (as they have recently learned) religious and cultural factors. For example, *sharia*, Muslim law, is now part of the verbal coinage of people who had not heard of it in 1999. A critical analytic mind seeking to understand controverted accounts clears some obstructions by asking what is included and excluded in a description; what explanatory principles are used and not used; what evaluations of the importance of factors are decisive; and what larger framework of meaning provides coherence to an account.

The opening illustrations in the first chapter were selected to force immediate recognition of this. Jonathan Edwards's description and explanation of the collapse of the Northampton church gallery was given in terms that would be acceptable to an atheistic construction engineer. The walls had been observed to be giving way; the underpinning had been considerably destroyed. Some persons "were buried in the ruins," and were "pressed under heavy loads of timber." These observations could be agreed upon by all parties. But Edwards, the Reformed pastor and theologian, also provided a theological interpretation of the same processes and outcomes: a divine providential intention determined the course and outcome of an event.

This was possible for Edwards, and for Calvin in his comments on differences in lactation, because the details of events were determined by the providential intentions of the sovereign God. It was also possible because Edwards had two distinct interests and perspectives, and the event was evaluated differently from each. Edwards, the close observer of natural events and their outcomes, valued a scientific explanation; Edwards, the Reformed pastor, valued the religious meaning of what was naturalistically explained.

Contemporary life is more complex than Edwards's. Few now are fixed on one or even two ways of interpreting events and responding to them. The same occurrences have several dimensions. Medical diagnoses and therapies have a primarily biological dimension, but also economic, moral, political, interpersonal, and spiritual dimensions. The same person, whether patient, health professional, or family member, has interest in more than one of them. Environmental crises have ecological, moral, political, economic, and spiritual dimensions. While one person might argue that the moral dimension is the key to change, everyone necessarily takes interest in more than one. The complexity of events and actions cannot be dissolved into unequivocal singularity by interpreting them from only one frame of reference, or from only one perspective, whether scientific, religious, or moral. Shifts from one perspective to another are common.

Some scholarly and other interpreters are convinced that one perspective provides *the* key to analyze an event, and thus is decisive in guiding an intervention into it. The anthropologist Franz Boas and his followers argued that cultural factors were most decisive in accounting for the potlatch ceremony; economists argue that the cultural factors were secondary to economic exchanges. If events entice or require a response from us, judgments are made about which perspective and dimensions are most accessible to guide effective interventions. Indeed, actions do not always follow from what is thought to be the "heart" of the issue, but from what is most practical—"actionable." A massive conversion from a consumer mentality to a spiritual, moral, or aesthetic one may be the heart of a matter from a religious or moral interest, but realism directs action toward legal, economic, and political means.

Christian activists and pastors face choices. Which perspective or explanation has privilege in determining the interpretation of a social problem or personal crisis? The answer is always context related. When theologians and moralists are engaged with clinical medical investigators or other physicians, the scientific perspective is primary. Pastors and moralists depend on the physicians for the description and explanation of a case. Any expansion of points to be considered from a religious and moral interest is not intelligible unless the scientific interpretation is accepted. Theologians and moralists are not competent to dispute scientific findings. To critically engage physicians, an enlargement of the interpretation of events and actions is required to show implications for moral and spiritual concerns. The major contribution of theology and ethics in interactions with scientific and other secular accounts is to expand the received information by interpreting it from a different perspective.

Again I emphasize that differences in accounts of intersections occur not only when religious discourse enters, but also when various secular disciplines and outlooks enter. Theology and ethics are not the only disciplines that confront the analytical agenda of this book. A sociobiologist or behaviorist psychologist will describe and explain a "moral choice" very differently from a rationalistic Kantian moral philosopher. To avoid a head-on collision, the Kantian will have to entertain an alternative interpretation of persons as moral agents as at least possible: the relation between biological drives and cultural conditioning on the one hand, and the capacity to govern actions according to reason on the other. The philosopher might concede that his colleagues explain *conditions* for action, but that moral acts require the positing of transcendental freedom to be explained. He may, or may not, be willing to admit that the scope of freedom has shrunk.[5] A sociologist or psychologist might argue that moral actions are simply the predictable outcomes of conditioning, even if they concede that the evidence is still inconclusive. Transcendental freedom is only a term that covers current ignorance.

Some accommodation might occur, but *integration* is possible only if one party grants that the perspective of the other is comprehensive and sufficient to explain and exhaust the meaning of the other. One discipline would have to replace the primacy of the other. Current efforts to *integrate* science and theology are ultimately futile. Only if the evidences, concepts, and modes of argumentation from a science account totally for religious discourse, or only if theology and other religious discourse determine the meaning of the sciences, would integration occur. In integration, if some theories and findings do not cohere they are often ignored or sublimated. A philosophical theologian, Alvin Plantinga, can propose "Augustinian science." But "integration" by a hard-line physicalist scientist will explain away theology.[6] Some form of accommodation is the most that can be achieved. Each form will differ, as the third chapter has demonstrated. Accommodation, at best, maximizes coherence and minimizes incoherence, and the meaning of traffic from each is revised to achieve this.

A shift in evaluative framework involves a reinterpretation of the meaning of events and actions. Edwards's theological explanation of the collapse of the gallery gave a very different meaning from his naturalistic one. Its meaning was related to his religious convictions about the nature of providential intentionality and its determination of natural outcomes. This returns, then, in a widely circular motion, to the root issue of this book. Do naturalistic explanations determine the possible religious and moral meanings? If not, are there no limits to possible theological interpretations of naturalistic accounts? The religious meaning always depends in part on theological convictions, or the general religious outlooks of participants. It will be relative to different theologies or religious communities. Self-critical awareness of how events and actions are reinterpreted by religious ideas and symbols is important. Most readers will reject Calvin's theological interpretation of differences in lactation; they have accepted a biological explanation. Calvin's observation that some mothers have sufficient and others insufficient milk, an observation about nature, does not warrant his belief that God wills some infants to be deprived. Awareness of how other received theologies are revised in the light of secular knowledge is the pedagogical purpose of this book.[7]

The distinctions among description, explanation, evaluation, and meaning have a heuristic function. They are useful to sort out where differences between religious and secular accounts are located. One can understand more precisely the reasons in various authors for rejection, absorption, or accommodation of secular to religious interpretations.

Mapping and Evaluating Differences in Outcomes: Rejection, Absorption, Accommodation

The first chapter indicated various ways in which the main issue of this book is avoided by Christians. I will, at this point, focus on the two current theological and religious movements that are oriented toward rejection. The rejection strategy takes two different theological forms, both with high visibility in American religious thought and church life. Both attempt to limit, if not completely obstruct, any effect on theological discourse of traffic incoming from the sciences and other secular knowledge. Neither *inter*acts with the cultural circumstances in which Christian theologians, pastors, and others exist. Both only *re*act to them.

One is Christian conservatism: fundamentalism, conservative evangelicalism, and Pentecostalism in Protestantism, and the radical traditionalist movements in Roman Catholicism. That there are significant differences in these movements is patently clear; generalization must be circumspect. What warrants including them in a group is the degree of rejection of any religious and theological significance of the sciences and other secular discourse. In most respects, these movements deny any necessity to alter or abandon some biblical and traditional beliefs in the face of evidences and theories that might refute them. Various indicators—"Christian television," megachurch growth, astute lobbying against the teaching of evolution and use of abortion and other items—mark significant growth in their numbers and influence. Many groups, of course, are very astute in adopting high technology and various modes of communication to their purposes: satellite broadcasting over the earth, current popular music styles, humor and other forms of entertainment, elaborate sets for performances, talk shows with prominent guests, fund-raising techniques, and so on. Secular writers are more forthright in pointing out dubious claims of healing miracles, obscurantisms, and inconsistencies in these movements than mainline theologians and pastors. In my judgment, Protestant theologians, moralists, pastors, social reformers, and liberal Roman Catholics need to define themselves more forcefully and effectively against the resurgence of these rejectionist movements than they do against "liberalism."

The other alternative is theological and ethical projects that make wholesale attacks on "modernity," "the Enlightenment project," "liberalism," and "foundationalism" in the names of "unapologetic theology," "postliberal theology," "narrative theology," and "narrative ethics," and various relatives of these. Proponents of this alternative have exploited various philosophical critiques of uncritical metaphysical and epistemological realisms, and various "postmodern" fads, to avoid ramifications and implications of secular interpretations for a whole range of Christian doctrines and theological ethical ideas.

In a time and place in which scientific and other secular knowledge provide dominating descriptions and explanations of actions, events, and other phenomena, and in which historic religious traditions cannot avoid intersecting with them more frequently, both fundamentalism and "postmodern" theology make it possible for Christian discourse to insulate itself from critical assessment by current intellectual and social movements. They expound views that raise doubts in the minds of many Christians, and are unintelligible to secularized persons. The first, more conservative alternative simply asserts positions on the basis of the heteronomous authority of the Bible. In the second alternative, theology and ethics can become academic disciplines in which authors address one another at learned society meetings in concepts and arguments that are arcane to secular scholars, and to many pastors and other Christians. The church moves toward Troeltsch's sect-type, disengaged from the culture and the dominant trends of its environment, or relates to them only as a countercultural critic—presumably a "prophetic" one— and *not as an engaged participant* in the determination of courses of events. Religious discourse can become defensive, vigorously attacking the idolatrous dogmatisms of others, yet unwilling to be as critical of itself as it is of secular knowledge, or to acknowledge alterations that have been made in its own beliefs while vigorously attacking idolatrous dogmatisms of others.[8]

Axiomatic to this book is this: it is not possible to avoid intersections between the sciences and other secular knowledge on the one hand, and religious discourse on the other. Nor is it possible to assimilate, or even accommodate, aspects of modernity such as astrophysics, neurosciences, molecular biology, many social and behavioral science findings, and many literary and artistic sources into "the biblical view" and traditional theology without altering the received tradition. What are "out there" as intellectual and academic issues are also personal: "in us," our minds and spirits and activities.[9]

A rejection strategy is wrong, or at least inadequate, for several reasons. First, it underestimates the cultural pervasiveness and persuasiveness of scientific and other secular interpretations in the culture in which Christianity exists. Even authors who fault "modernity" and "the Enlightenment project" have probably not expelled how it affects their daily lives: how they interpret political, social, medical, and other events and experiences. By positing the discussion "out there" in cultural generalizations and intellectual debates between radical universalization and historical particularity, they avoid confronting issues "in us" as persons and communities who are Christian and participants in the culture of the twenty-first century. Even if ministerial students, graduate students, theologians, and pastors are persuaded that modernity ought not to compromise theology and Christian belief, they have not uprooted modernity's influence on themselves and on most Christians. Christians do not confront "modernity" in some reified ("essentialized") form that at a high level of generalization can be criticized from an equally general view of a Christian particularism. They confront it in how events are interpreted by news commentators as well as political and social scientists, in pastors' use of evidence and insights from psychology as they counsel, in evaluating choices as consumers, in interpreting both the tensions and the blessings of their interpersonal relations. There is no escape from "modernity," whether it is attempted by fundamentalist recourse to the authority of the Bible on matters of history and nature as well as sin and salvation, or by sophisticated "postmodern" critiques of the sciences.[10]

Second, it tends to immune the Bible and Christian theology, beliefs, and practices from critical inquiry and analysis by the sciences and other secular discourse while being aggressively critical of much of modern thought and culture. Fundamentalists do this by tightly circular reasoning: belief in the verbal inspiration of the Bible by God confirms its accuracy of the creation accounts and other events, and thus its sure and certain grounds for rejecting evolutionary theories and other things. Others do it by demonstrating the errors of social and other sciences in their interpretations of religion and human faith. The authority of the sciences and other secular discourse is thereby qualified; their grounds for criticism of religion are shaken. Arguments that show the relativism of scientific and other secular knowledge weaken their authority; they are not as "objective" and "value-free" and comprehensive in their explanations as has been claimed. They have leaps of faith. They are also "particularities," just like Christian faith and theology. In fact, however, both fundamentalism and "postmodern" theology and ethics proclaim selected aspects of the Bible and theology.[11]

Third, without positive engagement with scientific and other secular accounts of texts, events, and actions that religious discourse addresses, academic theology and Christian beliefs are arcane to secularized intellectuals and to skeptical, commonsense people. A justification for religious beliefs and practices only on bases of revelational authority or critiques of excessive explanatory claims by the sciences is insufficient in contemporary culture. The former confesses a heteronomous authority; the latter involves Christian theologians and others in intricate historical and philosophical debates. Efforts to make Christianity intelligible, if not persuasive, and to probe secularists' equivalents of Calvin's *sensus divinitatis* are sometimes criticized for their vagueness. Awe, wonder, the sense of dependence, and so on are, in my judgment, not foreign to Christians, and are shared by other religious persons and by reflective, sensitive, secular people.[12]

Of course, theology and ethics written primarily for academic theologians and for the edification of the Christian community is important. There are many examples, such as expositions of the Trinity and the sacraments. Careful study of Jaroslav Pelikan's five volumes, *The Christian Tradition: A History of the Development of Doctrine,* informs learned theologians and refreshes their memory of arguments in the church about the sacraments, Christology, the significance of Mary, and other church teachings.[13] Pelikan is clear about his purpose; he has written a history not of theology but of Christian doctrines. A history of theology would entail accounts of the historical and intellectual, as well as ecclesial, circumstances in which Christian teaching develop and change, and the biographies of persons who developed them. The very internality of Pelikan's magnificent achievement determines both its contribution and its limitation.[14]

A similar confinement of systematic theology and ethics hones the intellects of scholars and students—for example, an explanation of the relations of the persons of the Trinity to one another—but leaves theological and religious discourse sounding arcane to secular people, and even to many devout Christians. One feature of Karl Barth's *Church Dogmatics* that maintains its significance is his interaction in section after section with secular discourse that addresses the same actions, events, and phenomena that he does. His theology is not isolated from its historical and cultural context, even if its authorization is special revelation. For example, in a discussion of sexuality Barth engages D. H. Lawrence's novels and T. van der Velde's "marriage manual," which was his contemporary equivalent of Alex Comfort's *Joys of Sex* and *More Joys of Sex.*[15]

Fourth, the rejection strategy is more satisfied than it ought to be with cognitive dissonance between religious and secular discourse in many intersections of beliefs and activities. It accepts too easily what Edward Farley calls dualism, or the ghost of Mani. Habitual ways of uncritically shifting from traditional religious language to scientific and secular accounts pertinent to the same phenomena are not a serious problem. Intellectually sophisticated ways of justifying cognitive dissonance abound among academic theologians: for example, the Wittgensteinian fideists' incommensurable language games and recovery of ancient views of double (or quadruple or quintuple) truths as in natural and revealed knowledge. Academic ways of resolving or accepting cognitive dissonance are not persuasive to many inquiring adolescent catechumens, college students, and self-critical participants in the life of the churches. To resolve cognitive dissonance "out there" in learned journals and books does not resolve it "in us," exposed as we all are to alternative interpretations of the human, historical and natural events, and texts. I dare say that for many Christians even to raise the issue causes uneasiness they wish to avoid.

Fifth, it gives religious and theological warrants for a sectarian view of the church. Christian ethics become fidelity to the teachings of Jesus, the pattern of his life and crucifixion, in moral action. It is not engagement in institutions and groups that are enmeshed in complex political and other spheres in which moral action cannot be justified by a single historically paradigmatic person or a single moral principle. Christian ethics becomes an ethic of pure conscience; if an ethic of social and cultural responsibility coexists with it, it is either an aggressive "prophetic" critique of dominant culture or an ethic of an exemplary community in the midst of a turmoil of prudential choices and compromises. It is averred that the church fell at least as early as Emperor Constantine by accepting a political and social order, and most religious institutions and communities continue in that heresy. To observe that this tendency toward sectarianism as inadequate, however, does not eliminate its commendable radicality in manifesting a moral rigorism and biblical fidelity, its critique of easy moral compromises and insufficient concern for particular Christian identity. An "over-againstness" is one, but not the only, necessary component of all church life.

This leads to my final observation, a theological one, about some, not all, rejections proposals. A conviction that God is the source and ultimate orderer of all created things entails conscientious participation of Christians in institutions and movements that powerfully direct current political, economic, social, military, and cultural events, the uses of nature and science and technology, and undramatic daily activity in work, leisure, and family life. The natural law as being morally ordered by God in Roman Catholicism and historic Anglicanism, the "orders of creation" in Luther's ethics, the Protestant doctrine of calling, the "mandates" described by Bonhoeffer, and many other Christian religious and moral formulations all emphasize theologically the creative and ordering work of the Deity, and the obligation of Christians to be participants in contemporary media of it. Because God is the ultimate ordering power, Christians, like all others, willy-nilly participate in the ordering of social and political life and human interventions into nature. Christians are to seek to discern and enact what the divine ordering enables and requires them to be and to do in their involvement in interpersonal, social, cultural, political, and natural life. An ethic that leans toward rejection in the name of Christian particularity denies many implications of a doctrine of divine ordering and creative activity.[16]

The absorptionist response to scientific and other secular knowledge that intersects religious discourse is also inadequate. It skirts the danger of assimilating and integrating religion and morality, theology and ethics, into a comprehensive scientific explanation of life. I have shown how the work of Philip Hefner, among the theologians analyzed, is most illumined by this type. I also mentioned various scientists, for example, E. O. Wilson, Richard Dawkins, and Steven Weinberg, who absorb religious discourse into scientific accounts to explain away its credibility. Edward Farley's turn toward phenomenology, especially the writings of Emmanuel Levinas, accounts for human experiences of freedom and responsibility that physicalists believe are, or eventually will be, explained fully by the sciences. But, as shown in chapter 3, Hefner never argues that religion and morality are explained away, even though they develop out of evolutionary needs.

The rejectionist tendency contributes grounds for radical critiques of scientific and secular culture. The absorptionist tendency opens paths for Christians who desire some reconciliation of their scientific and secular outlooks with their Christian faith and loyalty to the church. There is no way of knowing what percentage of Christians this is. Anecdotal evidence, however, confirms that significant numbers of educated Christians overcome some cognitive dissonance by reading Hefner and similar authors. There is no single point on a continuum between E. O. Wilson and Richard Dawkins on the one hand, and Hefner on the other that Christians—theologians, pastors, and laypeople—will unanimously agree is the limit beyond which Christian integrity is disastrously compromised.

A further contribution of an absorptionist tendency is its facilitation of discourse between theologians who are properly persuaded of the importance of engaging scientists, and especially those who have at least a sense of the divine. For many decades Protestant theology in a "neo-orthodox" phase focused on history more than nature as the arena of divine activity. The *Zygon* group did not number among its participants the most prominent Protestant theologians, and was sometimes viewed as a reductionist enclave. Interactions between theologians and scientists vary, however, in the degree of theological, scientific, and philosophical rigor, and can even issue in apologetic for traditional religious beliefs. Or the published literature is adapted by intellectually feeble, but spiritually enthusiastic, "New-Agers." Also, like all groups with a focused interest, concepts, terminology, and even in-group humor, it can be difficult for even an informed newcomer to participate.

Purveyors of traditional Christian interpretations of life can ridicule the unsophistication of a generous melding of religion and science into new spiritual and theological directions. But a sense of the divine, of awe, or mystery that motivates the confluence cannot be ignored. Calvin's *divinitatis sensus* is widespread among many persons who have rejected institutional religious life. Many books and articles have been published that express and address a sense of the sacred. Many are written by nontheologians, and read by many Christians as well as persons who have been put off by traditional doctrinal language. Superficial assimilation of such literature by church leadership is always a temptation.[17]

Cultured despisers who read Schleiermacher's *Speeches,* for all of their classic romanticism, can be strangely moved to acknowledge that they have similar religious and moral sensibilities. In a seminar that included a biophysicist, radiologist, primatologist, and persons from other parts of Emory University, Erazim Kohak's *The Embers and the Stars: A Philosophical Inquiry into the Moral Sense of Nature* was carefully read. Scientists who long ago had intellectually abandoned their Roman Catholic catechetical instruction, their institutional Judaism, and their Protestant Sunday school teachings resonated deeply to Kohak's religious, moral, and aesthetic sensibilities, though his phenomenological approach had no scientific grounds in their judgment. One cannot read through Melvin Konner's *The Tangled Wing: Biological Constraints on the Human Spirit* without being moved by his chapter "The Sense of Wonder." After several hundred pages to show the biological basis for human activities, Konner writes that we "must try again to experiences the human soul as soul, and not just as a buzz of bioelectricity, the human will as will, and not just as a surge of hormones, the human heart not as a fibrous, sticky pump, but as the metaphoric organ of understanding." Theodosius Dobzhansky, after a brilliantly lucid scientific account of the human, *Mankind Evolving*, ends with deep appreciation of Teilhard de Chardin's thought. Biologist and Presbyterian church member Ursula Goodenough narrates a scientific explanation in each section of *The Sacred Depths of Nature* and then beautifully meditates on it in religious, moral, and aesthetic terms. Wendell Berry's poetry, which at one point describes aging as "life steadily accumulating its subtractions," blends a profound human meaning into a biological process. All of these move from the biological. But they are not completely absorptionist; they do not integrate theology and religion into scientific explanations. They are accommodations from an absorptionist aspiration that open to wider horizons.[18] Theologians and pastors ought not dismiss such writings as theologically or philosophically naïve, or ignore their wide readership. To do so is to avoid traffic from modern culture that is open to the Divine.

The lure of the absorptionist ideal-type is almost inevitable to any Christian nature lover, and to theologians or moralists who stress that God is the ultimate creator and orderer of the universe. Precedents for this emphasis can be found in the Bible and through the history of Christian thought and piety. Although often revised and debated, explanations of the origin of the universe and the ordering (or disordering) of nature come from scientific cosmology, historical geology, and evolutionary interpretations of the origin and development of life. They include accounts of catastrophic natural events that do not confirm a providential process culminating in the existence of humans, or a romantic ultimate harmony of all things. A theology of the first article of the Apostles' Creed cannot ignore scientific interpretations of the origins and development of the universe—nature, or the creation, in theological terms.

Most theologians, moralists, pastors, and other Christians are somewhere between the extreme types of rejection and absorption. Most accept self-consciously or tacitly some accommodations in intersections of life and thought where secular and religious traffic meet. In the first chapter I made a distinction within accommodations. For some, scientific and other secular accounts *limit*, but do not determine, religious interpretations. Evolutionary sciences, for example, explain processes and events that intersect with a theology of creation.

Theologians do not substitute religious interpretations for scientific ones. They set a limit for what can be claimed theologically, but do not determine theological accounts of the meaning of life, and especially human life, as dependent on God—the power and powers that have brought life into being and determine its ultimate destiny. Farley's interpretation of the human is a case in point.

For others, scientific accounts *authorize*, but do not determine, theological interpretations. Inferences from the sciences authorize the trajectory and preferred evidences for a theological interpretation of life, but do not exhaust it. As has been shown, Barth sharply limits the significance of secular interpretations of the human; indeed he rejects any theological significance on the basis of his christological center of theology. Then, in light of that Christology they can be reinterpreted theologically. The evidences and explanations become symptoms of the real human, known only in Christ. Hefner, more than Farley, finds in the sciences an authorization for the basic trajectory and preferred language of his theology of the human, but these do not fully determine, that is, exhaust, what he expounds. Farley aspires to overcome the dualism between biology and theology. The sciences limit what can be claimed by theology but they cannot account for human intentionality, self-determination, and intersubjectivity. Hefner uses the sciences to show dependence of these features on nature, but other sources are also used in Christian theology.

Few, if any, Christian thinkers use only one criterion or rule to direct the flow of traffic In any intersection where theology and ethics meet scientific and other secular traffic. Interest in different Christian doctrines determines which secular traffic has to be directed, as I have shown above. Accommodation to traffic from astrophysics is different from accommodation to psychoanalysis: the former, prima facie, intersects with the doctrine of creation, the latter with theological anthropology.[19]

One point of uneasy accommodation is in the knowledge of God. Can God be a person with intelligence, will, the capacity to intend, command, and act, and who loves each human being, in face of interpretations of the origins of the universe and of human life as these are explained by the sciences? Or is the Deity the impersonal orderer of the physical universe, the biological processes, and the ultimate end (*finis* and *telos*) of all things? Does one have to concede that the power and powers that order much of life are impersonal, so that one says with Abraham Lincoln, in the context of the Civil War, that "the Almighty's purposes are his own"? Is the idea of God as person a projection from the human so that God is conceived in the image and likeness of the human? Is the impersonal view of God a projection from observations of nature? Or can an impersonal divine ordering be accommodated to a biblical idea of a God who acts, that is, as is an agent whose intellect and volition direct powers that affect discrete events and persons?

Bases for both interpretations can be found in the Bible. Both have been noted throughout the history of Christian thought and piety, but often in uneasy accommodation. Justin Martyr accommodated theology to secular philosophical accounts. Augustine used many pages in *The City of God* to distinguish a Christian interpretation of the sovereignty and providence of God from Roman fatalism. The ethics of Thomas Aquinas are developed not on the basis of a God who gives special commands in each instance of choice, but on the basis of the divine ordering of nature, including the nature of the human. A personal command of God was an extremely rare event in which God contravened nature, as in the "suicide" of Samson. Franciscan moral theology allowed for a moral occasionalism of discrete commands in particular circumstances. Luther and Calvin had to arbitrate conceptually the tension between human freedom in the image and likeness of God on the one hand and determinism, the ultimate divine determination of persons and events, on the other. In Jonathan Edwards's *Freedom of the Will* and *Treatise on Original Sin* one finds another complex accommodation. Changes are rung over and over between an ordering of life that *permits* but does not *cause* sin and evil—unavoidable phenomena—and thus exempts God's accountability for them. All of these are accommodation strategies in which the secular limits, but does not determine, a theological claim.

Which pole takes precedence deeply affects paradigms of theological ethics. Barth's stress on God as person, who graciously commands particular persons to act in particular ways in unique occasions, is opposite from Catholic ethics grounded in the divine moral ordering of nature, from which prescriptions and proscriptions can be adduced. God as person reasonably issues in ethics of God speaking and humans hearing, God commanding and humans obeying, God acting in events and humans responding to divine action. The dominance of God as an ordering power through nature reasonably issues in ethics in which humans infer from the divine moral order the laws and precepts that conform to it. Most Christians concerned with environmental problems implicitly or explicitly rely on an impersonal ordering and not divine commands, no matter what they believe to be the biblical interpretation of God.[20]

On this issue the question is similar whether Augustine is showing the errors of Roman fatalism or Freeman Dyson is answering the question, "Why Is Life So Complicated?"[21] But there is a historical difference. What was to Augustine and many others a metaphysical problem of freedom and determinism is now more complicated in three respects: the scientific accounts of an impersonal ordering are more complex and explained more precisely than a single word, *determinism,* suggests; these accounts, with their dynamic and complex interpretations, qualify a simple either/or choice between them; and popular media and education expose the explanations to more than the intellectual elite who read philosophy and theology.

One purpose of this book is to evoke in its readers a self-consciousness of how much traditional religious discourse has been altered by historical and contemporary sciences and other secular interpretations of the world. Another is to stimulate self-critical awareness of readers of their own accommodations and provoke reasons for them. The experience is "in us" as Christian theologians, moralists, pastors, and laypersons, and not only "out there" in scholarly journals and books.[22] Nothing in this book charges anyone with deliberate dishonesty, self-deception, or deception of others. There is no single rule that applies to all intersections that can mechanically prejudge the careful work of theologians, the theology and ethics that inform clergy in their preaching, pastoral care, and moral action, or that resolves the conflicts in the minds of college students. Our culture affects what are serious theological questions at any given time, and what answers are found acceptable. The trajectory and agenda of the classic forms of liberal Protestant theology are alive even in the Christian coroners who have certified its death.

I cite once more a cogent observation made by Paul Capetz in *Christian Faith as Religion: A Study in the Theologies of Calvin and Schleiermacher*. To compare their work at one point he wrote,

> The two epochs of Protestant theology must be understood as responses to distinct religious crises in the theological tradition of Augustine: the Reformation and the Enlightenment. From the Reformation to the Enlightenment there was a shift in the religious question itself from a concern with personal salvation from sin and guilt to a concern for the place and significance of human life within the comprehensive order of nature.[23]

This comparison does not imply that both of these Reformed theologians did not address both religious questions. Schleiermacher's consciousness of absolute dependence has affinities with Calvin's articulation of the awesome sense of dependence of all things, and particularly the human, on the power and majesty of the Creator. Also Schleiermacher, given his systematic and comprehensive coverage of Christian doctrines, interprets sin and guilt. In our time there are more comprehensive and detailed scientific and other secular accounts of the human in the cosmos, and even guilt, if not sin, than was the case in 1830. Scientific accounts of the limits of moral accountability, of conditions that lead to evil acts and guilt, affect Christian ethics and practices. Spinoza's writings provided a powerful secular philosophical interpretation of the world that was one context of Schleiermacher's theology and ethics. Thus his difficulty with the imagery of God as person, and his theology of the impersonal forces that determine much of the world.[24]

Rereading some writings of Ernst Troeltsch has helped me to focus the problematic outlook of this book. In his various reflections on the possibility of a liberal Christianity, a Christianity that might survive, if not thrive, in a scientific and secularized culture, he brought to attention especially three factors;

historical relativism as an undeniable aspect of Christianity, the relation of Christianity to other religious traditions, and the impact of the sciences on understanding of the world. Like Hefner, Farley, and others, the religious question for him could not be answered by deductive logic from scientific theories, but these questions had to be addressed by theology. "The idea of God is admittedly not directly accessible in any other way than by religious belief. Yet it asserts a substantial content which must stand in harmony with the other forms of scientific knowledge, and also be in some way indicated by these."[25] I would only amend "harmony" to "critically self-conscious relationship to. . . ."

Paul Tillich in his *Systematic Theology* wrote:

> Of course theology cannot rest on scientific theory. But it must relate its understanding of man to an understanding of universal nature, for man is part of nature and statements about nature underlie every statement about him. . . . Even if questions about the relation of man to nature and to the universe could be avoided by theologians, they would still be asked by people of every place and time—often with existential urgency and out of cognitive honesty. And the lack of an answer can become a stumbling block for a man's whole religious life.[26]

If Christian discourse is not to become an internal dialogue among persons who agree on a limited context, the thought of Schleiermacher, Troeltsch, Tillich, and others in the tradition of liberal theology must be heeded.

The authors of *Habits of the Heart* created a composite woman, Sheila Larson, who syncretistically developed her own religion, which they call "Sheilaism." Troeltsch noted the possibility that by absorbing and accommodating (my terms, not his) scientific knowledge and other religions into a Christian interpretation, at some point one might have a religion no longer identifiable as Christian—a Sheilaism. There is probably a bit of Sheilaism in most contemporary Christians who interact with a scientific and secular culture: some aspects of traditional Christianity are rejected or at least ignored, others have been reinterpreted as traffic from secular knowledge comes forcefully and speedily into religious lives and thought. My own direction of the traffic, in *Ethics from a Theocentric Perspective*, considered at least heterodox if not heretical by some critics, is only one position that can evoke critical reflection by others. Most theologians, moralists, pastors, and laypeople in our culture have explicitly or implicitly altered some aspects of traditional Christianity.

A theological precedent for this book can be found in many sources in the history of Christian thought. In chapter 1 I cited an authorization by Calvin. I repeat it.

> Whenever we come upon these matters [arts and sciences] in secular writers, let the admirable light of truth shining in them teach us that

the mind of man, though fallen and perverted from its wholeness, is nevertheless clothed and ornamented with God's excellent gifts. If we regard the Spirit of God as the sole foundation of truth, we shall neither reject truth itself, nor despise it wherever it shall appear, unless we dishonor the Spirit of God.

"The Almighty Has His Own Purposes"

From *Politics* to *Theology*

The title comes from Abraham Lincoln's Second Inaugural Address, delivered in March 1865, shortly before his assassination.[1] This chapter does not focus on different interpretations of Lincoln's life and career, or the Second Inaugural, except to make a point. The speech is not analyzed. It is not about Lincoln, but *from* Lincoln and his address. The address was given as the Civil War was nearing its bitter and bloody end. Lincoln reflected deeply in what Frederick Douglass, the intellectual former slave and abolitionist leader, said "sounded more like a sermon than a state paper." In my judgment Lincoln was America's greatest theologian of politics. His life and work were known well by the Niebuhr brothers: Reinhold, the most effective political theologian in the twentieth century, and H. Richard, whose articles on war published in 1942 have a pathos similar to Lincoln's address.[2]

There is a striking difference between Lincoln and the Niebuhr brothers, and all the major Christian theologians of politics from Augustine to our own time. Lincoln was *personally responsible* for conducting the government during the most internally critical event in American history, the Civil War. His theology of politics was shaped by the moral evil of slavery and the political and social upheavals that it evoked; by the more than half a million bloody deaths in combat, many of them the result of inept military leadership; by the many moral, legal, political, and military ambiguities in which he had to make decisions with no unequivocal choice. Lincoln's address represents one way of thinking theologically about politics: *from* historical events for which the thinker is deeply accountable *to* traditional Christian affirmations about God and the human. Lincoln spoke and thought not from Christian theology and its implications for understanding and acting in events, but from acting in events to traditionally accepted knowledge of God.

Reinhold Niebuhr was a persuasively astute *observer* and *analyst* of formative events in American history, and an articulate spokesman for social justice: in the era of "the business of America is business" in the 1920s as a pastor in Detroit, the automotive capital of the world; during the rise of Nazism in the 1930s; against liberal Protestant pacifism, and a proponent of the necessity of armed conflict against Hitler; the postwar period and international politics in subsequent decades; and much more. His observations about what would be required to overcome racism in America were prescient, made in 1928. Some commentators on recent events have brought the relevance of his work to attention, especially his *Irony of American History*. Reinhold Niebuhr moved *from* biblical myths, history, and concepts, from Augustine, Luther, Kierkegaard, and others in the Christian tradition *to* insightful analyses of economic conditions, political policies, and events; international relations, war and peace. His Christian faith assured Niebuhr of a fulfillment of hope: for love, justice, and peace "beyond tragedy." Lincoln's hopefulness was more circumspect. Niebuhr helps Christians use the narratives, theological concepts, beliefs, and outlooks of the Bible and Christian tradition to reveal deep currents and undercurrents of historical events. Lincoln forces Christians to test traditional Christian assurances in the light of tragic events and morally ambiguous actions. Niebuhr's Christian faith and theology assured him of forgiveness for choices made under realistic constraints, and of hope for the coming kingdom of God. Lincoln's experience saw a possibility for some redeeming outcomes of the Civil War, but he did not claim assurance of God's ultimate victory over sin, death, and evil in the coming kingdom of God. These are two different projects in political theology. In this chapter I follow Lincoln's path.

Why turn to Lincoln in the twenty-first century? Because I have had to meditate, brood, and think again about divine providence in light of political, social, and military events since the infamous date, 9/11/01; about the velocity and ambiguity of actions that have followed; about the foreseeable and unforeseeable consequences of choices being made in the United States and abroad. I cannot help but think about God during world events we have lived and are living through. Especially I have been compelled to examine how natural and moral evils have been theologically (i.e., verbally) "reconciled" with belief that God loves humanity and each person; the religious words that are used to sustain hope in the face of pitiful deaths and disfigurement from wars, starvation, and poverty. I have rehearsed in my memory writings from the tradition that have addressed issues of social and political order, of violence and powerlessness: Augustine and Thomas Aquinas; Luther; Michael Sattler, Peter Riedemann, and other Anabaptists; Zwingli and Calvin; the Puritans and Gerrard Winstanley, and others. I have reflected on the American theological penchant from the Puritans onward of asking, "What is God doing in historical and natural events?" I have reread the morally and religiously passionate articles by my mentor, H. Richard Niebuhr, written in World War II: "War as the Judgment of God," "War as Crucifixion," and in response to Virgil Aldrich, "Is God in the War?" "Yes" was his answer, but with a realism about historical accountability for the war not only by Germany and Japan, but also by American actions in the previous decades. Possible beneficial outcomes of the war were carefully stated. The articles come closer to a Lincolnian spirit than anything I have read. I have thought about Paul Lehmann, who, like H. Richard Niebuhr, said the first question of Christian ethics is not what is morally right and wrong about the aims and means of policies and courses of actions, but "What is God doing?" And particularly what is God doing "to make and keep human life human"? His most biblically and theologically elaborate account is titled *The Transfiguration of Politics*. I have thought about liberation theologians' use of the exodus motif, and of the coming kingdom of God. The theology of hope seems not to pass realistic examination in the face of actual and potential world events.

In the events on 9/11/01, some people claimed to know what God did and what God is doing subsequently. They have provoked me to meditate, brood, and think about Christian confidence in a benevolent and beneficent God who wills the well-being of humans. Claims to know what God is currently doing leave me with Lincoln, "The Almighty has his own purposes." They all mirror specific Christian beliefs and practices, and moral and political perspectives. This chapter is more the fruit of meditating, brooding, and thinking about the unavoidable, inherent, tragedies of human life and history than it is an academic analysis.

This chapter is *not an ethical analysis* of the current strife—whether a pre-emptive war is morally justifiable; whether the means used adhere to rules of the right conduct of a war, for example, noncombatant immunity (civilian children, women, and men in harm's way are now "unavoidable collateral damage"!); and whether the Christian response should be pacifist. I have read ethical analyses of the Afghanistan war, the war against terrorism, and the invasion of Iraq, some with all the refined intellectual sophistication of a traditional Jesuit casuist, some strongly critical of American actions, and some providing moral justification for them. The purpose of this chapter is not to make an ethical analysis, but to think theologically and passionately about the Almighty, whom Lincoln believed would prevail when both sides claim the high moral ground.

This chapter was first ventilated before an international audience assembled in Uppsala, Sweden. No occasion to deliver it occurred in the United States, which is significant because the entire world was occupied by the events of 9/11/01 and subsequent developments. Those events and their aftermath were, and are, still vivid in the memories of Europeans and others. The kind of events that provoke the most disturbing, haunting question about politics and God have occurred in every century of human activity, on every continent, in every historic culture. The outcomes of pain and suffering, of death and destruction, and of social disorder that follow violent events in which opposing sides have believed in the righteousness of their cause, if not the favor of the Almighty, will continue until our planet no longer sustains human life.

This chapter is not shaped by technical, theological, philosophical, historical, political, or other scholarly literature. It does not borrow theological authority to interpret events. Nor does it begin with biblical events and think analogously from them to current affairs. It cannot move from the transfiguration narrative in the Gospels to an understanding of what God is doing in current events to make and keep human life human, as Paul Lehmann did. It can find no analogy between the exodus of the Hebrew people from Egypt and current circumstances in which Americans and some Middle Easterners and Asians confront one another, each certain of the righteousness of their cause, as liberation theologians found analogies to Hebrew slavery and their exodus in political and economic oppression in the "Third World." It finds no moral or political insight from the kingdom of God for the conduct of relations between contemporary states and groups, whether in the mode of Walter Rauschenbusch or Jürgen Moltmann.

This chapter is not *out there* evaluating theological accounts for their intellectual and academic prowess to offer judgment, justification, or counsel. Nor does it emerge only from observations about other events that have been historically decisive. The issues are *in us*: in the responses of the heart, and not just the intellect, to devastation of societies and nature; to poverty, starvation, and despair whether experienced directly or through narratives and pictures; or to the dread of becoming victims of political, economic, and military choices by human powers beyond the control of those affected by them. The issues are in individual persons who reflect on circumstances, actions, and events that have affected their lives, their orientation toward other persons and the world, and their actions. To refute inflated religious symbolism, one sometimes hears, not every "crucifixion" issues in a "resurrection." The chapter comes not only from the study and thinking, but also from events in which I have participated and which I have experienced, not unlike those of readers, that have been thrust upon me over my lifetime.

On 8 August 1945, the day Hiroshima was bombed, I was in central Burma. I was a nineteen-year-old high-speed radio operator in a seven-man signal section of the Headquarters and Service Company of the 209th Engineer Combat Battalion. For communication with higher echelons in northern Burma and India, we had high-powered transmitters and receivers, and thus quickly heard news from All India Radio in New Delhi and Kandy, Ceylon. We were avid listeners to the reports of the bombing, including technical physical explanations by British scientists that none of us could understand. Our monthly beer rations had arrived that day by a DC3 landing at the Muse airstrip: twenty-four bottles per man. I and my reflective comrades (made more reflective as more beer was consumed) pondered the significance of the event. All but Fox and I had survived the seventy-eight day Battle of Myitkyina in the summer of 1944, when two engineering battalions building the Ledo Road were thrown in as infantry troops against a stubborn Japanese defense. Myitkyina had a strategic airstrip, and was the northern terminus of the Burmese railroad. I had replaced a man whose body was blown to bits by a direct artillery hit. We talked in barracks language in a clearing of jungle where our tents and equipment were located. Of course, there was joyful celebration! We had been told to expect two more years of war to dislodge the Japanese from China. This was the third monsoon season for the original members of the 209th. But celebration of victory did not totally overpower other reflections. What if the Japanese or Germans had built this strange new weapon before the United States had, and used it on an American city? The weeks in Myitkyina were vividly rehearsed, including memories of the man I had replaced. His mother had pitifully written to Captain Porter, the commander of H and S Company, to find out as much as she could about her son's replacement. Eberle's scar creased across his left temple was visible; his helmet had deflected a bullet that would have entered his skull. Johnson would occasionally still use a knife to dig out small bits of shrapnel coming to the surface of his body. We each remembered friends and classmates who had been killed in Leyte, or severely injured on Iwo Jima or elsewhere. Nothing we talked about was without some moral and human ambiguity, even though we were certain of the rightness of the American cause, and of our being soldiers. The success of that day in Japan, like every other one we talked about, was not without the costs of death and destruction to our enemies, and in this case to civilians. But this was not the first obliteration bombing both by the Axis powers and by the Allies. The ethical principle of double-effect (one is not morally culpable for the evil effect of an action that accompanies the good because it is unintended), which I learned subsequently, was unknowingly applied as we justified our joy in the face of death and destruction. The issues for us were not only *out there*—was rational justification possible?—but *in us*: our life experiences. Only later did I learn to ask, "Is God in the war?" Were the purposes of the Almighty his own?

Readers of this chapter, like me, have vicariously lived through the despair and unresolvable conflict in a friend or church member who finally chooses to end life because no pain and suffering being borne was less than any other; there was no available relief to contrast with the anguish. "Side effects" of medication to relieve depression, for example, symptoms of Parkinson's disease, can be as unbearable as the recurrence of insanity when the medications are terminated. Who dares speak ill of, not to mention morally condemn, such a friend or parishioner? Are the ways of the Almighty his own?

The issues of the previous chapters of this book are in us as well as out there. They are not merely intellectual and academic: Was the bombing of Hiroshima morally justifiable on the basis of the just-war theory? Is taking one's life under inexorably painful powers beyond one's control a case to be dissected by fine distinctions in a moral-theology textbook? Does *any* historical and other human evidence count against our teaching and preaching about a providential

Deity who provides redemption and hope to those in despair, to the people of nations devastated by decades of strife in Asia, Africa, or Central America? If God is gracious, is God also impotent to actualize those gracious purposes in natural and human-generated catastrophes? Is traditional Christian speech about redemption and hope a chimera when one observes or participates in suffering, destruction, and deaths of innocents—whether those are in New York City or Kabul or central Africa? Does God have preferences? Or are our accounts of God's preferences morally tainted by self-righteousness? Because Americans pray for their country and president, has God provided a protective "spiritual shield" under the "missile shield" for the safety of the United States? Or are our accounts tainted by our Christian tradition that is interpreted to say that God does prefer the poor and oppressed, even if the dominant evidences from natural and historical events are against that belief?

This chapter is in three sections, each of which has an epigraph. First, from President George W. Bush on the Sunday following the terrorist attacks on New York City: "God is not neutral." From the reports of the rhetoric of Osama bin Laden, he said the same. From religious commentators, both right and left, there was certainty.

Second, "God prefers the poor and the oppressed." We have heard this assurance over and over during the recent decades. Is it a historical social reality? Do the biblical evidences, the history of Christianity as a movement, and contemporary events, verify this? Or is it a normative statement of a Christian moral aspiration? If there is evidence against that presumed preference, is it all accountable to human sin? Or is it historically and naturally inevitable? If that is the case, how do we think about the Almighty?

Third, "The Almighty has his own purposes." One might begin with the biblical assurance that in Christ all things have been made new, or with reasonable deductions from a theological principle such as Barth's that "God is for Man," and have one view. One might begin with Lincoln's reflections on a costly war that was not yet over, and the outcomes of which continue to plague American history and society, and have a different view.

"God Is Not Neutral": George W. Bush and Osama bin Laden

It was Pascal who wrote that no man was more dangerous than an English Puritan with a rifle. No leader, whether from the United States or an Arab country, is more dangerous than one who is assured that God is on his side and he is on God's side: that his cause has the blessing of God; that the Manichees rather than Augustine were correct, namely, that history is a struggle between the unadulterated Good and the unmitigated Evil. And, unlike the relatively weak rifle of a seventeenth-century English Puritan with his rifle, now no one is more dangerous that one who has commandeered civilian jet aircraft that can be used as bombs, or threatens to use newly refined nuclear weapons.

The hazards of believing not just that God is on our side but that we are on God's side are palpable, as is the foreknowledge that such assurance can lead to devastating outcomes to both offenders and those offended against. Just as the political utopianism of the Soviet version of Marxism justified cruel and abusive means to achieve its end, so the belief that we are on God's side can warrant unrestrained pursuit against evil. It is difficult to limit destruction when a "crusade" has been announced.

Different voices claim to know what God is saying and doing in recent and current events. Pat Robertson and Jerry Falwell, two fundamentalist Christians with huge television audiences, believed that the terrorist attack was God's judgment against America for moral lapses and decline of religious practices. Of course, if changing sexual morality and the decline of religious practice would cause God's wrath to be turned on a nation, one might have thought that Sweden and most of Europe would have been God's target long ago! Those who know God's purposes from the radical Christian right wing are, for most readers of this book, easily dismissed.

But a synopsis of a sermon was sent me, preached in a liberal Protestant theological school two days after the event. If it was reported correctly, God was not neutral. The terror was God's judgment against the United States for our greed in globalized economies, our military imperialism, and our heedless exploitation of the earth's resources. Many persons agree that these are, at least, background causes of hostility toward the United States. Many ministers, however, quickly denied that a gracious God would use the violent deaths of innocent persons to judge America for its sins.

Is there any valid reason for believing that the second, a "prophetic preacher" in a theological seminary, knew the Almighty's purposes better than Pat Robertson and Jerry Falwell? Would the question be settled by citing biblical passages? By an argument over which sins are most putrid to the nostrils of the Divine? By pitting one theologian against another in an exegetical and doctrinal argument?

Quickly, for political reasons, President Bush and others assured the nation that Islam was not accurately expressed in the violence of the terrorists, and that we ought not indiscriminately judge that all who pray to Allah believe that Allah willed the violence. In effect, toleration of religious differences is necessary in an era of religious diversity, especially when some crucial allies are of another religious tradition. Though some name the Almighty "Allah" and others a Trinity, in effect, as Lincoln said, both "pray to the same God, and each invokes His aid against the other. It may seem strange that any man should dare to ask a just God's assistance in wringing their bread from the sweat of other men's faces. . . . The prayers of both could not be answered; that of neither has been answered fully. The Almighty has his own purposes." Not only is this the case, but our theologian of political events, in its light, cites Christian Scripture: "let us judge not that we be not judged." "Woe unto the world because of offenses! For it must needs be that offenses come; but woe to that man by whom the offense cometh." The ways of the Almighty are his own.

If that is the case, there is no unadulterated Good that warrants self-righteousness about a political cause. Lincoln, in Christian charity, believed that "the judgments of the Lord are true and righteous altogether," and that "as God gives us the right to see," both victors and defeated should bind the nation's wounds, care for those who have suffered from the battle, and "achieve and cherish a just, and a lasting peace among ourselves, and with all nations." But in almost a century and a half those Christian intentions have not significantly affected the course of human life and history. The wounds of slavery still pain millions of African Americans. Deaths by lynching are still in the memory of aging persons. There is no "just and lasting peace with all nations." Lincoln, like the Niebuhr brothers, sought hope beyond the tragedy. But Lincoln's realism was correct: the Almighty has his own purposes.

"God Prefers the Poor and the Oppressed"

Knowledge of this purpose of the Almighty has for decades been proclaimed not only by liberation theologians, Catholic and Protestant, but also by ecclesial officials, in much moving popular religious literature and preaching, and most commendably and impressively by social and moral action on the part of devout and dedicated Christians. During the 1960s my denomination, the United Church of Christ, had a liturgy at its national assembly that began, "God is an unmarried pregnant teen-age black girl on the west side of Chicago," hardly a theologically defensible statement, but liturgically moving to those present. One remembers the actions of black and white church people who marched and served the cause of civil rights in other ways. One remembers the assassination of Archbishop Romero and of the nuns and priests in El Salvador. The knowledge that God prefers the poor and oppressed motivated Christians to lead social protests if not violent revolutions, and to care sacrificially for the destitute victims of oppressive social, political, and economic forces who die on the streets, or live in refugee camps for fifty years. Mother Teresa of Calcutta led no revolts in East Bengal, a state governed for decades by Communists, but she did pray, "Dearest Lord, may I see you today and every day in the person of your sick, and, while nursing them, minister to you. Though you hide yourself behind the unattractive disguise of the irritable, the exacting, the unreasonable, may I still recognize you, and say, 'Jesus, my patient, how sweet it is to serve you.'"[3]

All readers of this book probably agree that one moral implication of the ministry of Jesus, of his death on the cross, and of the calling of the people of God is to prefer the destitute and oppressed, those suffering from starvation

and the aftermath of wars, the victims of AIDS and abuse, to the financial ty-
coons of Enron, the oil-rich rulers of the Middle East, and those who glory in
the triumphs of the politics and economies of Europe and North America. All
probably think that the Christian churches need to examine their pasts with
their Renaissance churches and temples now monuments more to art than to
the glory of God, the class biases of national churches that were often in league
with successful aristocrats and led proletariat families (like my paternal one in
Sweden) to find more hope and justice in Marxist parties than in Sunday high
masses and the hatefully memorized Luther's catechism. All probably now believe that the failure of theologians, pastors, and other male Christians to confront the oppressive domination of women entrenched in religious speech, civil
law, social custom, and ecclesial practice is so contradictory to the Christian
message that both repentance and restitution are required. Many probably now
believe that the purposes of the Almighty have been misread for centuries, and
that they are now realized through the restlessness of the oppressed, and the
aggressiveness of those who pursue the interests and rights of the poor. Maybe
many who believe that God prefers the poor would have in the sixteenth century sided with the peasants in the revolts in central Europe, with Thomas
Munzer and others, rather than with Catholic prelates' and Luther's certainty
that suppression was required.

By drawing selectively from the Bible, one can make an *ideal* theological
case and a *normative* ethical case that those who are faithful to God should prefer the poor. But interpreters begin with the narrative of Moses and the ancient
Hebrews' exodus from slavery in Egypt, and tend not to recall the beneficence
of Yahweh to the patriarchs with their thousands of cattle and slaves, or the assurances that righteousness is rewarded by prosperity, and even that the tragic
realist, Job, finally reaped earthly rewards. With more assurance Christians find
that the life and message of Jesus move Christians to identify with the oppressed, and that love and justice (which usually are now said in one breath) require support of social policies that protect the well-being of the powerless, the
victims of suffering imposed by powers beyond their control. Theologically, it is
argued that, to use Karl Barth's expression, "God is for man," and that to believe
this is to serve the needs of the human, and especially those who are "dehu-
manized" by poverty, war, social custom, and disease. Probably all Christians
agree that there is a moral imperative in the Christian faith and life to act self-
sacrificially to meet the needs of the poor and oppressed; and many agree that
Christians ought to support social and economic policies within and between
nations that prefer the poor. This is correct.

But does historical and social evidence assure us that God, who rhetorically
is claimed to be the Lord of history, the Redeemer of all, the one who has made
all things new in Christ, prefers the poor? Did Yahweh prefer the slaves of the
patriarchs to the wealth of their owners, as he preferred the Hebrew slaves to
their Egyptian overlords? Did the God who commanded the Hebrews to exter-

minate those who occupied the land promised to them show preference for their poor? Did Yahweh especially care for those who are widowed and orphaned as a result of that command? If David is among the saints of the Scriptures, does his behavior, his military and political success, support a divine preference for the poor? Do we argue that only Micah, Amos, and a few others knew God's purposes, rather than the priests with their temple sacrifices, or the foreign conquerors of God's children? Did the church begin to fall with the assurance of Clement of Alexandria that a rich man could be saved, and his prudent reminder that if there were no rich persons there would be no one to meet the needs of the hungry? Was God's purpose clearly known in the poverty of the first Franciscans but not realized in the wealth that the mendicant orders accumulated in two or three generation? Was John D. Rockefeller's deviously gained wealth contrary to his Christian faith, and his founding of the University of Chicago and other praiseworthy institutions contrary to his Baptist loyalty?[4]

Is there theological significance to the fact that I was born in a country at a time in its history that it has prospered beyond anyone's anticipation, and not in India or central Africa? That I was born in my generation, and not that of my father, who carried tools and water in the construction of the Klabböle Dam on the Ume River all during his tenth year? If God prefers the poor, why am I, my family, and countless others so fortunate?

If God prefers the poor, is the destitution, the deprivation, the pain and suffering of those millions whose plight draws our compassion due only to the human fault—sin? Or is much of it the outcome of historical and natural conflicts and forces beyond the capacity of any individual human, or any government, or any nongovernmental organization, to alleviate, not to mention eliminate? If God prefers the poor, is God impotent to fulfill that preference? Or is it up to Christians, and to non-Christians who often better marshal their powers, to actualize God's preference for the poor? But are not the limitations of human control over human destiny met in the details of resistance to the putative preference of God? Are frustration and defeat not *inevitable*, historically and naturally? It is clearly the Christian mission to prefer the poor and oppressed. But if that is a purpose of the Almighty, the Almighty is not Almighty. God may be love, but love is not God; love is not omnipotent—unless we proclaim the eschatological solution of a final reign of love and justice, unfortunately not realizable in the tragedies of historical life.

Can we live in the midst not only of catastrophes of history and nature, but also tragedies in which it is historically and naturally inevitable that the innocent suffer from forces beyond their powers, that those who are sure they are on God's side slay the innocent and disrupt the peace of nations in Asia as well as North America? Can I, who have suffered with the destitute vicariously more than actually, not wonder if God's preference for the poor and the oppressed is only some kind of generous wish, and not a divine intention actualized in human events and actions?

"The Almighty Has His Own Purposes"

Some interpreters of Lincoln believe his language, with its opening "malice toward none and charity toward all," affirms divine providential action in the events and outcome of our Civil War. Others interpret his language to be a more stoic necessity in the inevitably tragic character of life, if one thinks not in a Niebuhrian direction from Christian beliefs about the purposes of God, but in a Lincolnian direction from the tragic events to whether some traditional Christian beliefs can stand contrary evidence. Is God *the sovereign power* but not fully a *providential* power? Is the ultimate power ultimately good? (To many readers those are an adolescent's questions, asked of her confirmation pastor, to which he has answers—verbal ones at least. But the issue is not just doctrinal, conceptual, and logical; it is experiential, and our verbal answers often are hollow to human experience.) At least one scholar I have read suggests that the idea of necessity comes from a memory of Lincoln's mother's frontier Calvinism.

Maybe, if Lincoln's faith was Christian at all, it was a Christian *stoicism*—recognizing the inevitable tragedy of life with a strong hint of some modest hope for a better life. Or a *stoical* Christianity, like the Swedish piety in which I grew up: in face of deaths of innocents and destructions of nature and society, we consent to the harsh but unavoidable outcomes by saying that the Almighty has his own purposes. It is not ours to try to rationalize them with what we would prefer them to be. Nor is it ours to say what God intended. (This stoical piety may be more Swedish, or even northern Swedish, than Christian.) The purposes of the Almighty are his own.

In the face of memories both personal and social, and of events my generation has lived through, I am left with Lincoln: deep economic depression; my war—the Second World war—and subsequent dozens of them in all parts of the world; events full of promise, like the end of colonialism that I eagerly saw coming in India in late 1945 and early 1946, realized on 15 August 1947 only in untold bloodshed—and now so pathetically unfulfilled; the eradication of smallpox only to have the pandemic of AIDS; millions malnourished because, with surplus nutritional resources, human institutions are not organized to feed them; homelessness on city streets in Albuquerque and even Stockholm—the rehearsal could go on and on and on. In some decades before the onset of my old age, and now with less time devoted to ideas in books and more to brooding and reflecting on experience, though often vicariously, I ponder the inevitability of genuine tragedy: some values unfulfilled so that others can be realized; some evils restrained only for other evils to take their place. I am left with Lincoln: "The Almighty has his own purposes."

As a Christian stoic, or a stoical Christian, the life of the church and its Christian message and mission are part of my life. But I move from boredom to frustration to anger with the exaggerated religious rhetoric that makes promises that God probably cannot keep; assurances of a cosmic hope, but not much attention to the small possibilities for some tiny improvements in the complexities of individual, interpersonal, and public life; proclamations that all things are made new in Christ when nothing significant changes in human actions and events; the proclamation that God became a human and was crucified, and thus we are made free by grace only to be overwhelmed by the same anxieties and fears, remorse and guilt, that heard the proclamation; the self-assured religious hucksterism of American Protestant television preachers who with high technology conduct revivals around the world rejoicing in snatching individual souls from the fires of hell that none of them deserves; and worse, the claims that by touching my damaged shoulder to the hands on a screen of a taped television program it can be healed "in Jesus' name"!; and more and more and more. I move from boredom, to frustration, to anger.

Theologians have historic documents that rhetorically answer the queries of adolescents, old people, and others who feel a cognitive dissonance. There are idealistic ways—in ultimate reality the contradictions are solved; there are eschatological ways—when the reign of God comes all will be resolved; there are personal assurances—the evils and pains of this life will be relieved and even glorified in a life to come when we put off this mortal body and put on an immortal one. Ways are found via Derrida or Wittgenstein or others philosophically to justify traditional Christian orthodoxy, or at least ward off some criticisms of it, as if the intellectual and academic Zeitgeist of relativism secured the possibility of God revealing Godself in a particular person and event in a particular time and place. Preachers assure congregations that God really loves each individual, indeed that God is love *as if love is God*, and God is not all the other things God is in the prayers of St. Francis and Karl Rahner—wisdom, power, wrath, and ultimately with the Cappadocians and all great mystics since, the ineffable, the unspeakable, the unknowable.[5] Laypeople prefer familiar religious language, even though it creates cognitive dissonance between Bible-speak or theology-speak, or sermon-speak, or prayer-speak, and all the secular ways they always use first to interpret and understand actions, events, and ourselves. And some Christians revel in the assurance by theologians that they are resident aliens on this planet, who can criticize the culture but not be criticized by it.

A few years ago the eminent medical sociologist Renée Fox sent me a copy of a beautiful tribute to her mentor, the Harvard sociologist Talcott Parsons. She tells how Professor Parsons, in his discussions with her, said, "Renée, don't exaggerate."

> Politicians, don't exaggerate!
> Theologians, don't exaggerate!
> Social reformers, don't exaggerate!
> Christian clergy, don't exaggerate!

Politically and religiously exaggerated rhetorical claims to know the purposes of the Almighty exceed the bounds of human finitude. They are idolatrous. When George W. Bush assured the American people that God is not neutral, he meant not that God was on the side of the terrorists, but that God was on the American side. Religious moral rhetoric escalated so that the military action was—fortunately only for a few days—called "Operation Infinite Justice." Whatever "infinite justice" might refer to, it clearly claimed to transcend human, historical, and finite justice. The cause was infinitely just! To be infinitely just it must have the moral approval of the Infinite—God. To name the struggle a "crusade" brings memories of a Manichean view of events: the forces of unadulterated good against the forces of unmitigated evil; and of medieval Christian crusaders storming Islamic Constantinople and enjoying the spoils of war. There is no acknowledgment that the "Good" is also infected by duplicity, self-deception, self-serving motives covered by announced good intentions, and even schadenfreude; that violence against those who presume to be good may be motivated by unjust exploitation, cultural condescension, and the arrogance of power. The temperament of a crusade is righteousness about one's cause; it is difficult to restrain the use of available means to obliterate the evil. Thankfully, action is often more restrained than rhetoric. But, once assured of the justice and righteousness of a cause, one can overhear Martin Luther counsel that "in a war of this sort it is both Christian and an act of love to kill the enemy without hesitation, to plunder and burn and injure him by every method of warfare until he is conquered (except that one must be aware of sin, and not violate wives and virgins)."[6]

The exaggeration of political rhetoric, and its escalation into religious and theological rhetoric, is not hard to criticize when our moral and religious sensibilities are affected by blatant certitudes that one nation's cause is God's cause, that God's cause is being fulfilled by one nation. One can move in the direction of great political theologians, like Reinhold Niebuhr, to use biblical narratives and metaphors, and theological doctrines of sin, forgiveness, and hope beyond tragedy to interpret historical events in which we participate. One can see readily that the Christian tradition can illumine some of the deep dimensions of human experience of self-righteousness, of inflicting evil on others, and being the victims of evil inflicted by others. One can see that the outcomes of events are not fated, but provide at least some conditions of possibility for change to the better, that out of historical crucifixions at least some modest newness of life is possible. One can turn, with Lincoln, to Christian Scripture, and be warned that we should judge not that we be not judged, and that (like Luther, the Niebuhrs, and countless others) after the violence we should look for reconciliation and restoration, with malice toward none and charity toward all. Some might even hear in the American government's verbal assurance that it will help to rebuild a destroyed nation, once evil is eradicated, a faint echo of many Christians, Luther included, that once victory is achieved "mercy and peace" should be offered. Beyond destruction there is some hope of reconciliation, restitution, and renewal, indeed of a gracious redemptive activity.

It is more difficult and painful to be certain that God prefers the poor and oppressed: to be passionately convinced that pursuit of the well-being of the deprived is a mandate of the gospel and theology; and then to see poverty and oppression continue or even increase. It is painful to see that promises of liberation from colonialism still leave the liberated in starvation, wars, ethnic and communal strife, disease, and other destruction; that legal assurances of equal human rights have not markedly changed the social conditions of those whose rights the law secures; that in a world of abundance there continue to be vast discrepancies between nations and between persons and groups within nations; and the litany could go on and on. Lincoln's aspiration does express a Christian hope beyond tragedy: "[with] malice toward none; with charity for all; with firmness in the right, as God gives us to see the right, let us strive . . . to bind up the nation's wounds; to care for him who shall have borne the nation's wounds, and for his widow, and his orphan—to do all which may achieve and cherish a just, and a lasting peace, among ourselves, and with all nations." He did not live to attempt to turn this moral vision into policy; nor has anyone succeeded in doing so since. The ambiguities of every aspect of actions and events are never eradicated by hope, or even by commitments to the times and places when significantly better conditions are possible because of a Christian preference for the poor.

Lincoln, one might conjecture, would move from our contemporary events—even in the light of "firmness in the right, as God gives us to see the right" to bind up wounds, prefer the poor, the suffering, and the destitute—and reflect theologically as he did in those last weeks of the great tragedy of American history, that "the Almighty has his own purposes." Lincoln moved from the tragic events in which he was the major player to reflections on the Almighty. In a similar way I, and surely other Christians, have to move from the historical and social ambiguities and tragedies inherent in the movements of history and nature that are beyond human control, to reflect on the Almighty. I cannot fully account for those tragedies as the outcome of human sin—a factor that Lincoln recognized in the Second Inaugural—but the outcome of the sovereign powers and power that are beyond the capacity of all human will, technology, and institutions to fully determine. The Almighty has his own purposes.

God will be God!

Notes

Chapter 1

1. Jonathan Edwards, "Letter to Isaac Watts and John Guyse, March 17, 1737," *The Works of Jonathan Edwards, 1834,* 2 vols. (reprinted, Edinburgh: Banner of Truth Trust, 1974) 1:345–46.

2. John Calvin, *The Institutes of the Christian Religion,* ed. John T. McNeill, trans. Ford Lewis Battles, 2 vols. (Philadelphia: Westminster, 1960) 1:201–2 (emphasis added).

3. Van A. Harvey, *The Historian and the Believer: The Morality of Historical Knowledge and Christian Belief* (New York: Macmillan, 1966).

4. Hans W. Frei, *The Eclipse of Biblical Narrative: A Study in Eighteenth and Nineteenth Century Hermeneutics* (New Haven: Yale Univ. Press, 1974).

5. Calvin, *Institutes,* 1:273–74.

6. George A. Lindbeck, *The Nature of Doctrine: Religion and Theology in a Postliberal Age* (Philadelphia: Westminster, 1984) 135.

7. Theological and religious scholarship follows the availability of funding sources no less than economic, political, or medical scholarship and teaching.

8. Alan Gewirth, *Reason and Morality* (Chicago: Univ. of Chicago Press, 1974).

9. Melvin Konner, *The Tangled Wing: Biological Constraints on the Human Spirit,* 2d ed. (New York: Holt, 2002).

10. Paul E. Capetz, *Christian Faith as Religion: A Study in the Theologies of Calvin and Schleiermacher* (Lanham, Md.: Univ. Press of America, 1998) 201.

Chapter 2

1. The publications of Gary Becker, Nobel laureate in economics, are an example. For an early collection of papers, see Gary Becker, *The Economic Approach to Human Behavior* (Chicago: Univ. of Chicago Press, 1976).

2. The more speculative writings of E. O. Wilson are an example. The best is *On Human Nature* (Cambridge: Harvard Univ. Press, 1975). My review of this book was titled "A Secular Systematic Theology" (*Hastings Center Report* 9:44–45).

3. See Alan Donagan, *The Theory of Morality* (Chicago: Univ. of Chicago Press, 1977).

4. Abraham Joshua Heschel, *Who Is Man?* (Stanford: Stanford Univ. Press, 1965).

5. Reinhold Niebuhr, *The Nature and Destiny of Man,* 2 vols. (New York: Scribner's, 1941–43), vol. 1: *The Nature of Man.*

6. Melvin Konner, *The Tangled Wing: Biological Constraints on the Human Spirit,* 2d ed. (New York: Holt, 2002).

7. Toni Morrison, *Beloved* (New York: Penguin, 1988).

8. Jonathan Edwards, *Freedom of the Will,* ed. Paul Ramsey (New Haven: Yale Univ. Press, 1957) 142. See pp. 141–48.

Chapter 3

1. See P. Travis Kroeker and Bruce K. Ward, *Remembering the End: Dostoevsky as Prophet to Modernity* (Boulder, Colo.: Westview, 2001) iii.

2. John Milbank, *Theology and Social Theory: Beyond Secular Reasoning* (Oxford: Blackwell, 1990).

3. Ibid., 260.

4. Ibid., 259.

5. E. O. Wilson, *On Human Nature* (Cambridge: Harvard Univ. Press, 1975); Patricia Smith Churchland, *Neurophilosophy: Toward a Unified Science of the Mind-Brain* (Cambridge: MIT Press, 1986). See Robert N. McCauley, ed., *The Churchlands and Their Critics* (Oxford: Blackwell, 1996).

6. Samuel Kincheloe, a sociologist of the urban church, liked to point out that to assist a person to drive from Hyde Park in Chicago to San Francisco you had to explain the intricacies of driving from 57th Street and Woodlawn to US 30. In his southern Ohio accent he often told theological students, many of them new converts to process theology, "If it ain't local, it ain't real."

7. James M. Gustafson, *Treasure in Earthen Vessels: The Church as a Human Community* (New York: Harper and Brothers, 1961).

8. Paul M. Harrison, *Power and Authority in the Free Church Tradition: A Social Case Study of the American Baptist Convention* (Princeton: Princeton Univ. Press, 1959). The distinguished British theologian Bishop Stephen Sykes cited Harrison's book recently in my presence as a "classic study" of the kind of analysis he commended.

9. George Appleton, ed., *The Oxford Book of Prayer* (Oxford: Oxford Univ. Press, 1985) 115.

10. Hefner, Ted Peters, and other Lutherans whose work on science and theology I know were taught by process theologians at the Divinity School of the University of Chicago.

11. Philip Hefner, *The Human Factor: Evolution, Culture, and Religion* (Minneapolis: Fortress Press, 1993).

12. Ibid., 27.

13. Ibid., 75.

14. Ibid., 81.

15. Ibid., 57.

16. Ibid., 58.

17. Ibid., 60.

18. Ibid., 62.

19. Ibid., 133.

20. Campbell, quoted by Hefner, *The Human Factor,* 134.

21. Hefner, *The Human Factor,* 136.

22. Ibid., 141.

23. Ibid..

24. Ibid., 86.

25. Ibid., 87.

26. Ibid..

27. Ibid., 178.

28. Ibid., 184.

29. Ibid., 189.

30. Ibid., 190–91.

31. Ibid., 193.

32. Ursula Goodenough, *The Sacred Depths of Nature* (New York: Oxford Univ. Press, 1998).

33. Gordon D. Kaufman, *In the Face of Mystery: A Constructive Theology* (Cambridge: Harvard Univ. Press, 1993), especially 97–111; Edward Farley, *Good and Evil: Interpreting a Human Condition* (Minneapolis: Fortress Press, 1990).

34. Farley, *Good and Evil,* 77 n. 4.

35. Ibid., 77.

36. Ibid., 78.

37. Ibid..

38. Melvin J. Konner, *The Tangled Wing: Biological Constraints on the Human Spirit,* 2d ed. (New York: Times Books, 2002); Mary Midgely, *Beast and Man: The Roots of Human Nature* (Ithaca: Cornell Univ. Press, 1978).

39. Farley, *Good and Evil,* 81–82.

40. Ibid., 82.

41. Ibid., 79.

42. Ibid., 87.

43. Ibid., 95.

44. Ibid., 113.

45. Ibid., 244.

46. Karl Barth, *Church Dogmatics,* III/2 (Edinburgh: T. & T. Clark, 1960) 71–132, and 132–202.

47. Ibid., 72.

48. Ibid., 73.

49. Ibid., 74.

50. Ibid., 77.

51. Ibid., 80.

52. Ibid., 85.

53. Ibid., 87.

54. Ibid., 88.

55. Ibid., 90.

56. Ibid., 94.

57. Ibid., 109.

58. Ibid., 125.

59. Ibid., 127.

60. Ibid., 135.

61. Ibid., 160.

62. Ibid., 198.

63. Ibid., 199.

64. Ibid..

65. Ibid., 202.

66. In June 1990, I led a seminar for a day on the intersection of disciplines with the faculty of the Department of Human Sciences and Revealed Knowledge, at the International Islamic University, Kuala Lumpur, Malaysia. Scholars were from biology, political science, economics, sociology, psychology, and humanities, including philosophy. Discussions of intersections between fields were learned, engaging, and mutually respectful while also being critical. It was clear, however, that the Koran and Islamic tradition would determine the perimeters and parameters of any comprehensive and coherent interpretation. Traffic from religious thought would determine the course and the boundaries when secular scholarship merged with it.

67. For my more thorough analysis and commentary on Barth's ethics, see *Christ and the Moral Life* (New York: Harper & Row, 1968) passim; and *Ethics from a Theocentric Perspective,* 2 vols. (Chicago: Univ. of Chicago Press, 1981–84) 2:26–42.

68. George A. Lindbeck, *The Nature of Doctrine: Religion and Theology in a Postliberal Age* (Philadelphia: Westminster, 1984) 135.

Chapter 4

1. I was once asked by a group of Lutherans to comment on a very early draft of a statement on death and dying. The formula was conventional: the biblical basis, the theological basis, ethics, and application. I noted that there was no reference to the biblical idea that death was caused by sin. The first response was that we do not know whether that means physical or spiritual death. I pointed out that Luther, in his lectures on Genesis, believed God condemned Adam to death, and thus all of his descendants, although he also wrote about a "translation" from physical to spiritual life. The second response was that the phrase would have to be demythologized, which the purpose of the statement prohibited. After much discussion, my final comment was, "Why don't you say that death is caused by degeneration of the body, and not by sin, and tell Lutherans that they don't have to believe that anymore? Most of them probably don't anyway, and might be relieved that they don't have to."

2. The final chapter narrates my thinking about tragic events in human experience, in the light of divine providence.

3. Those of us who studied sociology of knowledge and sociology of religion in the mid-twentieth century are astonished by the excitement of "postmodern" theologians and other scholars when they discover the relativity of knowledge to the interests of particular institutions and groups. For some of us this was a fact of experience in multiethnic, multidenominational communities, and in Asian countries during World War II, before we knew any theory.

4. Elsewhere I have called this "philosophy of theology" comparable to the philosophy of science. Philosophers of science need not focus on particular sciences, e.g., genetics. Philosophers of theology need not focus on particular doctrines, e.g., redemption.

5. I read an account by Mark Wallace ("Barth, Derrida and the Language of Theology, *Religious Studies Review* 25:349) of five books on Jacques Derrida and Karl Barth, most of which find in Derrida's "postmodern" critiques a philosophical justification for Barth's radically particularistic confessional theology. Since I have read dissertations on Barth and Kant, Kierkegaard, Heidegger, Wittgenstein, and others, I suspect that Derrida provides a currently correct authorization for Barth's project. My mental response was, "I always thought that Barth's theology, ethics, and preaching were authorized by God's revelation in the Bible, and especially in Jesus Christ—not by philosophical authority borrowed from a current academic Zeitgeist." The power and integrity of Barth's revelational claim evokes my respect more than philosophical justifications for its possibility. I wonder if any preacher whose is informed by Barth's theology is more confident because it has a "postmodern" backing, or if any congregation is more persuaded by the preacher.

6. Some of my publications, but more by my students, were motivated by the lack of intellectual rigor in Protestant ethical writings. Indeed, one attraction of Roman Catholic moral theology is its refined distinctions and rational arguments. A manuscript reader of the first volume of my *Ethics from a Theocentric Perspective* criticized it because there was no introductory chapter on methodology.

7. Similar observations can be made about how pastoral theology and other work intersect with secular studies.

8. H. Richard Niebuhr's constructive, or ideal, typology of Christ and culture could be used heuristically throughout this book. "Christ against culture" illumines the wider significance of the stance of Milbank and Hauerwas and Ochs. Troeltsch distinguished between two postures of "against" groups: to be an exemplary community, and to be an aggressive prophetic community. Stanley Hauerwas's writings have elements of both. See H. Richard Niebuhr, *Christ and Culture* (New York: Harper and Brothers, 1951).

Differences in theological contexts are illustrated by the following personal experience from my student years. In January 1949, I represented the then-flourishing Chicago Interseminary Movement at a large Christian student conference at the University of Kansas. Enthusiasm for ecumenism was high shortly after the 1948 Amsterdam Assembly of the World Council of Churches. Divisions between churches were manifestations of sin. The fact that, as I recall, three different denominations had church buildings on the same corner in Lawrence was evidence. My effort to mitigate the accountability of sin by proposing social and historical explanations was deemed theologically "shallow" by very "neo-orthodox" students from Yale Divinity School, Union (New York), Princeton, and other seminaries.

9. Edward Farley, *Good and Evil: Interpreting a Human Condition* (Minneapolis: Fortress Press, 1990) 97.

10. John Milbank, *Theology and Social Theory: Beyond Secular Reasoning* (Oxford: Blackwell, 1990) 260.

Chapter 5

1. I vividly recall Wilhelm Pauck's final words at the end of a 1951 course on theology since Schleiermacher, "Barth has not answered Troeltsch; he has only bypassed him."

2. I am acquainted with technical philosophical and cognitive psychological literature on perception, *Erklärung und Verstehen,* and other concepts that refine the analysis of interpretation. I am not interested in evaluating theories, only in suggesting terms for heuristic purposes.

3. This is based on discussions with my late friend Peter Aranson, an Emory University economist.

4. The seminar was under the auspices of the Midwest Section of the American Academy of Arts and Sciences, which I chaired at the time.

5. This debate took a vigorous and rigorous form in a discussion between a moral philosopher and a biologically oriented anthropologist. It ended in an agreement to disagree.

6. The cognitive psychologist Ulric Neisser always concluded in our discussions about theology, "Jim, there's nothing there."

7. Since the Thomistic account of natural law is suffused with Aristotelian biology, an intriguing thought experiment is how the insertion of contemporary scientific biology in place of the Aristotelian would affect the ethical implications. A major frustration in my career occurred when a Canadian nurse with advanced degrees in biology and theology proposed to write a dissertation on this. Both a human geneticist and a philosopher of science agreed that she was uniquely equipped, but in the face of colleagues who required her first to formulate her metaphysics she left in frustration. Stephen Pope has subsequently written in this vein. His approach was to criticize Roman Catholic personalistic, or existentialist, accounts of love as inadequate for making discriminating decisions about how love applies to particular circumstances. In effect, he infused contemporary biology into St. Thomas's account of the order of charity. See Stephen J. Pope, *The Evolution of Altruism and the Ordering of Love* (Washington, D.C.: Georgetown Univ. Press, 1994). Stephen G. Post analyzed *Christian Love and Self-Denial* in American Puritan theology, including Edwards (Lanham, Md.: Univ. Press of America, 1987). He continues to attend to specific human circumstances, e.g., care of Alzheimer's patients, in which love and care are required. See, for one example, *Spheres of Love: Towards a New Ethic of the Family* (Dallas: Southern Univ. Press, 1994).

8. My critique is based not only on an interpretation of our historical situation, but also on a theological conviction about the sovereign power of God. See *Ethics from a Theocentric Perspective,* 2 vols. (Chicago: Univ. of Chicago Press, 1981–84). If God is sovereign, and Christians are called to serve God, involvement in secular affairs is mandated that requires openness to rethinking Christian beliefs and practices.

9. My wife and I worshiped in an Atlanta Presbyterian church on a Sunday when the preacher enthusiastically expounded themes from *Resident Aliens: Life in the Christian Colony,* by Stanley Hauerwas and William H. Willimon (Nashville : Abingdon, 1989). I walked from the sanctuary with a lawyer whom I had met who was a candidate for a congressional seat in a primary election. He said to me, "Can you imagine Atlanta Pres-

byterians as resident aliens?" From this social observation one might extrapolate a theological significance. Heirs of the Reformed tradition, among others, cannot be satisfied with a sectarian rejection of, or aggressive counterculture posture toward, the society and culture in which we live. Like the lawyer, they are called to participate in the ambiguities of social and political life not by absorbing the world into the biblical view, and not by finding an epistemology that authorizes particularistic Christian ethics and theology. Participation entails openness to alterations in some ethical postures and beliefs.

10. I once asked a European theologian how he travels across the Atlantic so frequently, after a lecture in which he argued that Christians, especially, should strip back their use of technology to at least a sustainable level. Certainly not by wind power.

11. In a session in which my wife and I were considering membership in a congregation, another inquirer asked where the minister and the denomination stood on activities about which there are clear divine commands, particularly abortion and homosexuality. The pastor's "I like the one about tithing" was too subtle for him.

12. I have described "senses" that are general among human beings in *Can Ethics Be Christian?* (Chicago: Univ. of Chicago Press, 1975) 92–114; in *Ethics from a Theocentric Perspective*, 1:129–36; and in "Say Something Theological!" the eighth annual Ryerson Lecture delivered to an audience of University of Chicago faculty and students in 1981, and published by the University of Chicago Publication Information Office.

13. Jaroslav Pelikan, *The Christian Tradition: A History of the Development of Doctrine*, 5 vols. (Chicago: Univ. of Chicago Press, 1971–89).

14. At Helsinki University, Finland, I spent several hours with a philosopher whose detailed knowledge of medieval literature on Mariology, Christology, the Trinity, the Eucharist, and moral theology overwhelmed me. His interest, however, was in the logic of the arguments, which in its symbolization was unintelligible to me, but important to logicians, e.g., the deontic logic of Fransciscan moral theology.

15. Karl Barth, *Church Dogmatics*, III/4 (Edinburgh: T. & T. Clark, 1961) 134–39. I recently heard, for the first time, a mass by Leoš Janáček. After its first performance in Prague a critic wrote that Janáček apparently had gotten religion in his old age. Janáček, it is reported, sent the critic a postcard, "Not old. Not religious." In the Credo the text moves from the virgin birth to the crucifixion, accounting for thirty-three years in one sentence, "He was made man." Janáček, at that point, provides a quite lengthy orchestral interlude. I heard it as an atheist's sarcastic reminder of what confinement to traditional orthodox creeds ignores.

16. My interpretation of a theology of a divine ordering and its ethical implications is developed in *Ethics from a Theocentric Perspective*.

17. In a Lenten study series in which I taught, classes were offered in the passion narrative in Mark's Gospel, the death penalty, examples from historical Christian ethics, etc. A class in tai chi attracted the largest number of participants.

On a visit to a church conference center in which there is a small Zen garden and a labyrinth, I inquired about the construction of the latter. I was told that there are precedents in the medieval church for their use by Christians. I responded, "There are precedents in the medieval church for burning heretics, too." So much for the selective use of historical precedents to justify assimilation.

18. In a review of John Polkinghorne's *The God of Hope and the End of the World*, for which he received a Templeton award, the theoretical physicist Freeman Dyson, also a

Templeton laureate (as one such now identifies himself in print), wrote, "I am a practicing Christian, but not a believing Christian" ("Science and Religion: No Ends in Sight," *New York Review of Books,* March 28, 2002).

19. In his first quarter as a professor at the University of Chicago Divinity School, Seward Hiltner conducted a seminar on psychology and ethics. The point was to prove the experiential implausibility of Paul Ramsey's newly published *Basic Christian Ethics* (New York: Scribner's, 1950). Ramsey interprets Christian love as "disinterested love for the neighbor," following Luther, Nygren, and especially Kierkegaard. Hiltner, I am sure, focused on such sentences as, "If a person has love for his enemy-neighbor from whom he can expect no good in return but only hostility and persecution, then *alone* does he become certain that he does not simply love himself in loving his neighbor. If you wish to assure yourself that love is disinterested, you must remove every possibility of requital" (pp. 98–99, italics added). He commends Kierkegaard's example of love of the dead as a test. "Christian love means such love for self [including feelings, emotions, preferences, temperament, and other qualities] is inverted. The standard of Christian ethics is drawn from the human *only* by inverting it" (italics added). "Thus Christian ethics draws its standard *from man* only by inverting it" (p. 100). The other major book was by a psychoanalyst and was used to show the psychological naïveté, and therefore the moral impossibility, of Ramsey's position. Psychology gave evidence that inverted self-love is impossible.

20. One of the challenges and delights of my teaching career at the University of Chicago was leading college students, most of whom had no religious instruction or were from non-Christian traditions, through Luther's 1536 *Lectures on Galatians* and Calvin's *Institutes*. One aim was to inform them about perennial issues in Christian theology that other instructors addressed differently. On a January morning at 8:30, I met nine students in a very cold room in the Political Science building. The assignment for that session included a passage from Calvin in which he refers to God both as an impersonal orderer of nature and as an active agent. I was greeted by an excited young woman who virtually shouted, "Mr. Gustafson, John Calvin can't have it both ways!" My effort to explain how Calvin, like scores of theologians, accommodated the two were to her verbal games to avoid a logical contradiction.

21. The argument of this chapter in Freeman Dyson, *Infinite in All Directions* (New York: Harper & Row, 1988), could be a syllabus for a rigorous encounter with the sciences by theologians, students, pastors, and others.

22. "In us" refers not only to individuals but also to families and friends. Many readers have radically secularized children and grandchildren whose vocations exercise more self-denying compassion and action for the poor and oppressed than that of most orthodox believers. For some, Judaism, Buddhism, Islam, and Hinduism are not reified religious traditions to be studied comparatively, but the faiths of family members, friends, colleagues, and neighbors. Should these religions be rejected, absorbed, or accommodated by traditional Christian theology? They are personified in persons who are loved and admired. Does the fact of personal accommodation by Christians to Jews, Hindus, Muslims, and secularized persons call for a self-conscious theological justification? If it does, what aspects of biblical and traditional theology are rejected, or radically reinterpreted, e.g., Karl Rahner's idea of "anonymous Christians," or Karl Barth's distinction between being graced by God de jure and de facto?

23. Paul E. Capetz, *Christian Faith as Religion: A Study in the Theologies of Calvin and Schleiermacher* (Lanham, Md.: Univ. Press of America, 1998) 210.

24. See Julian Lamm, *The Living God: Schleiermacher's Appropriation of Spinoza* (University Park: Pennsylvania State Univ. Press, 1996).

25. Ernst Troeltsch, "Religion and the Science of Religion," in Robert Morgan and Michael Pye, eds., *Ernst Troeltsch: Writings on Theology and Religion* (Atlanta: John Knox, 1977) 117.

26. Paul Tillich, *Systematic Theology*, 3 vols. (Chicago: Univ. of Chicago Press, 1951–63) 3:5.

Chapter 6

1. During the course of preparing this chapter two very relevant books about Lincoln were published: Ronald C. White, *Lincoln's Greatest Speech: The Second Inaugural* (New York: Simon & Schuster, 2002); and William Lee Miller, *Lincoln's Virtues: An Ethical Biography* (New York: Knopf, 2002). I encourage my readers to read the address and meditate on it. Both authors are theologically trained. Less recently I have pondered Garry Wills, *Lincoln at Gettysburg: The Words That Remade America* (New York: Simon & Schuster, 1992); and Allen C. Guelzo, *Abraham Lincoln: Redeemer President* (Grand Rapids: Eerdmans, 1999). These join thousands of books about Lincoln. Even though they are hagiographic, I have read Carl Sandburg's five volumes several times. Lincoln was my immigrant father's American hero.

2. H. Richard Niebuhr's 1942 articles in the *Christian Century* are most accessible in Richard B. Miller, ed., *War in the Twentieth Century: Sources in Theological Ethics* (Louisville: Westminster John Knox, 1992): "War as the Judgment of God" (pp. 47–55); with Virgil C. Aldrich, "Is God in the War?" (pp. 56–62); and "War as Crucifixion" (pp. 63–70).

3. In Tony Castle, compiler, *The New Book of Christian Prayers* (New York: Crossroad, 1987) 224.

4. It is interesting to see in a biography of Walter Rauschenbusch how Rockefeller found ways to support his fellow Baptist, the social prophet, who also found ways to accept Rockefeller's aid. See Paul Minus, *Walter Rauschenbusch: American Reformer* (New York: Macmillan, 1988).

5. Francis of Assisi: "You are holy," "strong," "great," "Most High," "almighty," "King of heaven and earth," "Three in One," "good, all good, supreme good," "love," "wisdom," "humility," "endurance," "rest," "peace," "joy and gladness," "justice and moderation," "all our riches," "beauty," "gentleness," "our protector," "our guardian and defender," "our courage," "our haven and our hope," "our faith," "our great consolation," "our eternal life," "Great and wonderful Lord, God Almighty, Merciful Saviour." See ibid., 135–36.

Karl Rahner: "What can I say to you, my God? Shall I collect all the words that praise your Holy Name? Shall I give you all the names of this world, you, the Unnameable? Shall I call you 'God of my life, meaning of my existence, hallowing of my acts, my journey's end, bitterness of my bitter hours, home of my loneliness, you my most treasured happiness'? Shall I say: Creator, Sustainer, Pardoner, Near One, Distant One, Incomprehensible One, God both of flowers and stars, God of the gentle wind and of terrible storms, Wisdom, Power, Loyalty and Truthfulness, Eternity and Infinity, you the All-merciful, you the Just One, you Love itself?" In George Appleton, ed., *The Oxford*

Book of Prayer (Oxford: Oxford Univ. Press, 1985) 361. The complete text is in Karl Rahner, *Prayers for a Lifetime,* ed. Albert Raffelt (New York: Crossroad, 1987) 4–8.

6. Martin Luther, "On Temporal Authority," in "The Christian in Society II." *Luther's Works,* ed. Walther I. Brandt (Philadelphia: Muhlenberg, 1962) 45:125.